Career Lessons
From Mentors and Tormentors

By Joseph James Pestka

© 2022 by Joseph James Pestka

All rights reserved. This book or any portion thereof may not be reproduced or used in any manner whatsoever without the express written permission of the publisher except for the use of brief quotations in a book review.

ISBN: 979-8-218-02614-1

Table of Contents

Introduction · vii
Special Thanks ·xi
Foreword ·xiii

Chapter 1	The Cook ·	1
Chapter 2	Simon Says ·	5
Chapter 3	Agricultural Duties · · · · · · · · · · · · · · · ·	9
Chapter 4	The Mall Experience · · · · · · · · · · · · · ·	15
Chapter 5	The River Rat · · · · · · · · · · · · · · · · · · ·	19
Chapter 6	Everyone Gets One Pass · · · · · · · · · · ·	23
Chapter 7	Good Time Charlie · · · · · · · · · · · · · · ·	27
Chapter 8	Shuffle Along Stanley · · · · · · · · · · · · ·	31
Chapter 9	PJ ·	33
Chapter 10	Slim Felice ·	35
Chapter 11	The Carpet Crew · · · · · · · · · · · · · · · · ·	37
Chapter 12	The Pare ·	39
Chapter 13	The Dodger ·	41
Chapter 14	Scottie Boy ·	45
Chapter 15	Michael Me Lad · · · · · · · · · · · · · · · · · ·	47
Chapter 16	Queenie ·	49
Chapter 17	Tony the Head · · · · · · · · · · · · · · · · · · ·	51
Chapter 18	Skeeter Bomb! ·	53

Chapter 19	Rudy	55
Chapter 20	Jimmy the Greek	59
Chapter 21	Big Jim	63
Chapter 22	Old Hickory	77
Chapter 23	The Louisville Crew	79
Chapter 24	It Ain't Easy	83
Chapter 25	Big Ron	85
Chapter 26	The Cowboy	89
Chapter 27	The DOS	93
Chapter 28	The GM	99
Chapter 29	The Opposite	105
Chapter 30	I'm Loving It!	107
Chapter 31	Shaky, Not Stirred	109
Chapter 32	The Bullet	111
Chapter 33	The OC	115
Chapter 34	My Father, Joe Pestka Sr.	117

Closing........125

Introduction

I followed my father into the trade show business. Well, I somewhat followed him. One day he told me it was time to grow up, and I found myself working with him.

Following family in the trade show business was common for many people when I started. If you weren't related to family, it was a friend that brought people into the business.

The trade show business used to be a hidden industry, and it would have been difficult to choose a career path in it without having a connection to have known about it. There was another reason there would be several members of the same family in the business. As a relative brought you into the business, you already knew there would be long hours, as you had watched your relative work those long hours before you started. Working long hours and weekends would not come as a surprise to you.

Another reason so many members of the same family were in the business was that whoever brought you in, your performance was personally accountable to that relative.

Looking back, I feel lucky to have followed my father into the business. I was also lucky to have worked with a unique group of people over the years and have made a few observations that I am sharing in this book.

Regarding the origin of the title of this book. I have not consulted with Webster's to confirm the definition of a mentor, which leaves me to write about mentors from my perspective.

Typically, most people think of mentors as the people who take the time to explain things and guide you along. Mentors might even provide guardrails to keep you in the correct lane. As you'll find while reading this book, and as I did living it, mentors may also be the people one might observe doing something well that you pick up on, and then you just do what they did. In some cases, they also show you what not to do.

Tormentor is just a play on words.

Tormentors might be the people who push or create adversity for you. Like everyone else, there have been times when I was pushed out of my comfort zone and overcame adversity. What matters is how you react to the situation. You grow as a person when pushed without breaking, and, if you pay attention, you might learn a lesson from it.

The point of this book is that you can learn and benefit from almost everyone around you and the more observant you are the more you will pick up.

The idea for this book came from an experience I wrote about in my first book, "Dad Lessons."

While at dinner with my family when my children were younger, I shared some of the names of the people I worked with and a short story about them. My children couldn't believe the names of some of these folks, and they were too young to appreciate the lessons I was sharing with them. My children are young adults now, and I hope they enjoy the stories a little more this time around.

The people I write about in this book were all good people, and considering the time I spent with them, many became great friends. They carried themselves well and had a sense of pride and achievement for doing a job well done. The people I write about earned respect every day by a job well done.

Writing the book reminded me of many more people that I didn't include in the book. I could have continued to write and include everyone; however, had I included everyone, this book may never have made it into publication. If this book does well, there might be enough people I didn't write about in this book to write a sequel.

Suffice it to say, over the course of my career I learned a lot from a lot of people.

The situations I have written about most likely took place a long time ago too. I can't imagine the environment is like it was anymore; a lot has changed.

I hope you enjoy reading about these folks and the lessons I learned as much as I enjoyed working with them, learning from them, and now writing about them.

Special Thanks

Special thanks to my wife Teresa and our children, Hunter and Madisyn, for being a wonderful family and for their patience while wondering if I would ever finish writing at night and on the weekends.

This is my second book, and in the first book, because of my inexperience writing books, and as I was in such a hurry to publish it, I did not include the special thanks to my wife and children in that book. The title of my first book is *Dad Lessons, from an Outrageous Dad*—so yes, go figure, how could I forget the special thanks for my family in that book! They have always known I love them and appreciate their patience, and now it is in writing!

Foreword
by Nicole Snyder

Do you work with someone who is a veteran in your industry, but who still strives to learn and take something away from each day? I can honestly say that I am *not* this person. While I do love to learn and take something from each day, I often find myself in a spot where I cannot find that silver lining when I am in a tough situation. I can get caught up in details and lose sight of the big picture. It is easy to do, right? However, I am quite fortunate to have friends who are able to find a lesson in each day, and they, albeit unknowingly, have shown me that I can shift my mindset and better face each challenge at work as an opportunity for growth.

I'm fortunate enough to have worked with Joe for almost twenty years, and I can say that he is someone who is able to look at a situation, pull out the facts, decide what needs to be done, and let go of what he can't control. He can remove emotion from a situation and try to find a lesson or a famous quote to best capture the situation and encourage everyone to move forward.

This book is a great encapsulation of the many lessons Joe has learned over the years. Even in the most difficult situations at work, there is always something or someone that we can learn from. Sometimes the lessons also make you laugh! I know a few of the chapters in this book sure gave me a chuckle! Being able to take away a lesson from even the most unlikely of characters is something perhaps we should all strive for.

These stories remind me that sometimes you just need to pause and reflect on the situation and see what lesson you can take away. Not every situation is dire, though it may feel that way at times.

As Winston Churchill said, "Success is not final, failure is not fatal: it is the courage to continue that counts." So if we have the courage to continue, perhaps we can also find the courage to try to find the lesson in each day.

1
The Cook

My first job with a paycheck was washing dishes at the local Chinese restaurant. I was fifteen, and the pay was the minimum wage of $3.35 per hour. This is where I started.

This restaurant happened to be the gold standard for Chinese food in our town. To this day people still include it in their online group discussions as the best Chinese food around. I still go there occasionally for lunch or dinner, just not to wash the dishes.

Washing dishes is a hard job, and it's even harder in a Chinese restaurant. Chinese food is served on multiple serving dishes. You may not have considered this while you are out dining; I believe many current and former dishwashers consider this stuff.

I estimate this restaurant used about twice as many dishes compared to most other restaurants. Most midpriced restaurants serve the main course and sides on a single plate. Chinese restaurants serve the main course in a tin with a lid to keep it warm. The rice has its own bowl, then you place everything on a main plate from which you eat, and don't forget, there is a plate for the egg rolls. Each setting has a teacup in addition to your water and drink glasses; you are getting the picture now.

One of the negative consequences of washing dishes is that every pair of shoes you wear to work are ruined from the food falling on them while scraping dishes and the water overspray used to prewash the dishes.

One can only go up from their start of washing dishes.

Joe Pestka

The best part of the job occurred after we had closed and the customers were gone. After the dining room and kitchen had been cleaned up, we were served dinner. Everyone sat down at the biggest table in the dining room, and we ate together. It was a great team, and dining together was a fun way to end a busy night. My favorite dishes were the pork fried rice and the pork egg foo yong. I still order these dishes when I go there as a patron.

One particular cook made our dinner every night. I didn't know his name and he didn't know mine, but that didn't keep us from having a friendly but rather limited banter about dinner every night. His grasp of English went as far as what was on the menu and that was it. I didn't speak any Chinese, so I never had a clue what he was saying to me. At any rate, we pretty well knew what each other was communicating thru our friendly banter.

Our banter would start when dinnertime came around and we had to let the cook know what we wanted for dinner. I would request "dinner for six" or the "steak kow." The cook would blow a gasket when he heard my request! He would shake his head no, wave his arms, and yell things that had the other cooks laughing and I didn't understand. There may have been more to his message than denying my request, judging by his yelling, arm waving, and the reaction from the other cooks.

After the banter was over, I would order one of my two favorite dishes and we all sat down together and ate. The owners of the restaurant even joined us, and we enjoyed each other's company.

The cook was middle aged, and I think he began to tire of what I thought was our friendly banter, so he decided to end it. The time to order dinner came, and I asked for the steak kow and he smiled. No arm waving or banter. I thought maybe I had scored.

I went to the dinner table and waited for my steak kow. The cook emerged and handed me a big plate of chicken tails with an even bigger smile! There may be an actual name to describe this part of the chicken, but I don't know what it is. It was the arrowhead-shaped part of the chicken at the back end where the chicken's tail feathers would have been.

Everyone at the table was in on it, so there was a good laugh for everyone. The cook was a good sport about it too. He knew my standby favorites and handed me a plate of my usual once the laughter subsided.

The Career Lesson: When you are the dishwasher, you are at the bottom of the rung; don't ask for the dinner for six or the steak kow, as you haven't earned it yet. It might take chicken tails for you to understand this.

2
Simon Says

The trade show industry used to be a feast-or-famine type of business. When the shows were in town, they needed people, and between shows, there wasn't a need for people. As summer was busy in Chicago, it was feast time, and there was always an opening to work.

My father helped me to get hired on during summer vacation. At fifteen, I began my career in the trade show industry. This was before laws had been enacted that prohibited minors from working in industrial environments. I was now working during setup and tear-down on the show floor in McCormick Place. I commuted with my father to and from work, sleeping both ways on the commute.

My first position was to deliver rental furniture during setup days and then to retrieve it during move-out days during the production of the show. During setup before the show opened, my first task included rolling dollies full of chairs and tables onto the show floor, then unloading and placing the chairs and tables in booths for exhibitors to use during the show. Once the show was closed, we rolled the empty dollies back out on the show floor and placed all of the rental furniture back into the dollies.

On my first day working in McCormick Place, I was assigned to work with Simon as my partner. Simon was a few years older than I was, and he had been working there for a while, so he knew the job. Simon and I worked the entire day together without saying a word to each other that the other understood. Simon only spoke Spanish and I only spoke English. We weren't able to communicate verbally.

Simon was a hard worker and a good partner. As Simon had been working there for a while, he showed me the ropes. Despite our communication barrier, I learned the job from him. I would watch him do a task, and then I would just do what he was doing.

When it was break time, Simon would hold his hands up over his head as if he had a stick between them and pretend to break the stick. We both spoke that language, and we never missed a break.

As the show opening drew near, it became safe to deliver the more fragile equipment with less risk of it being broken. Back in those days, one of the more popular rental items were the smokers. Smokers were glass ashtrays affixed to wood and metal pedestals that were about twenty-four inches tall. As smoking was still permissible in the exhibit hall and still socially acceptable, exhibitors needed to provide ashtrays for themselves and the attendees in their booths to dispose of the ashes and butts from cigarettes and cigars.

As the new guy, I was number one on the list for delivering and retrieving the smokers. As I had a couple days working with Simon under my belt and had learned the ropes, I was on my own now. As Simon left me, he smiled, as I had this task. Simon went on to doing things that were more important.

Setting the smokers out wasn't a bad job, as they were clean and did not weigh too much compared to the tables and chairs we had been delivering. After the show closed, I found that picking up the dirty and stinky smokers was the payback. The ashtrays were dirty from the ashes, making this dirty work. I hope I never have to do anything like that again.

The actual task of retrieving the smokers included dumping the ashes and cigarette butts onto the exhibit hall floor, then returning them to the boneyard to spray Scrubbing Bubbles onto them. Once the scrubbing bubbles had soaked in, I then wiped the ashtrays clean. After they had been used a few days, the ashtrays had a hard coating of ashes that proved to be difficult to clean off too. Contrary to what they said in the commercials, the bubbles were not doing the scrubbing for me, so I had to scrub them. Once the smokers were clean, we would place the smokers back in their dollies for storage until the next event.

One might ask why we didn't dump the ashes and butts from the smokers into one of the wastebaskets on the show floor that we had rented to the exhibitors. I look back, and I didn't think twice about dumping the ashtrays onto the floor while I was doing it. After all, there were wastebaskets all over after the show, and we could have easily thrown the ashes into the wastebaskets.

The last thing we picked up during move-out were the wastebaskets, and then we just dumped the contents of the wastebaskets onto the exhibit hall floor as well. We would not have achieved anything if we had emptied the ashtrays into the wastebaskets; it would have just delayed it from ending up on the floor. It's crazy to think how it all just ended up on the show floor back then.

Fortunately, smokers are not rented, and they are no longer needed.

Simon is still working in the same department as he was back then. He mostly leads crews or is on a forklift now.

Now, when Simon and I see each other, our communication has improved a great deal. We start with a handshake and transition to a hug in one motion. After our embrace, we say hello and ask how each other is doing. After that, it falls back to our early days together pretty quick with a lot of smiling and nodding and then back to a handshake, a hug, and a see-you-later.

I always enjoy and appreciate seeing Simon.

The Career Lesson: Give an honest day's work for an honest day's pay, and whether you move up in the department or out of it, at some point you won't be the new guy forever and you will graduate from doing the grunt work, or in this case smokers and wastebaskets. With experience, you will move on to doing something more meaningful.

3
Agricultural Duties

During summer vacations while still in high school, and between working shows, I would travel to Great Falls, Montana, and stay with my uncles. I would fly into Great Falls in late June after the spring shows and return to Chicago in mid-August for the late summer shows. My uncles, Donald, John, and Mike, lived in Great Falls. My Uncle Donald worked in town for the city of Great Falls as a laborer, and my Uncles John and Mike traveled during the week to build and rebuild the roads throughout the state as operating engineers.

The summer after I turned sixteen, a friend of my Uncle Mike's, Dudley, who was a partner at an agricultural implement dealer in Great Falls, offered me a summer job. We were on a backpacking trip in the Bob Marshal Wilderness Area, and Dudley offered me the job for the rest of the summer I would be in Great Falls. I suppose I carried myself well enough hiking and camping that Dudley thought I would be helpful at his dealership.

My duties at the dealership included sweeping the shop floor, driving the tractors, combines, and yard equipment about a quarter mile to the fuel station to fuel the equipment, and delivering and picking up parts in town and around the surrounding counties. My favorite task was delivering agricultural equipment to farmers all over the state.

Every morning my Uncle Donald and I made our lunch, and then we went our separate ways to work for an 8:00 a.m. start. This job has been the one and only regular job I have ever had. I mean a regular job with regular

Joe Pestka

eight-to-five hours, Monday through Friday, with an hour for Lunch, for forty hours with weekends off.

While in Montana, I was wearing cowboy boots, a cowboy hat, and a big belt buckle; I looked as cowboy as any kid born and raised in Montana. My Uncle Frank, a retired laborer, had introduced me to Redman and Beechnut chewing tobacco, so I had that going too. There were a couple more stories with my Uncle Frank, but they weren't career related, so I won't include them. That summer I really lived it up being a Montana cowboy.

One day our task was to deliver a used combine to a farmer in Turner, Montana. The city of Turner is northeast of Great Falls and sits just a few miles south of the Canadian border. While on these deliveries, my role was to drive the pickup truck pulling the eighteen-foot-long trailer that transported the cutter for the combine. The cutter is the front part of a combine, which cuts the stalks of wheat, then sends the wheat to the main combine to separate the grain from the stalks.

During the delivery, while driving the pickup towing the trailer with the cutter, I would follow the semi truck pulling the trailer with the actual combine on it. For a suburban Chicago kid, this was an amazing summer job. I was able to see a lot of Montana, and as the fourth largest state, Montana has a lot to see.

When we arrived at this particular farm in Turner, Montana, the farmer directed us to a large, flat field away from his house and barn to unload the combine. Delivering the combine consisted of backing the combine down the ramp of the trailer and then driving it into position to attach the combine to the cutter. After we had attached the combine to the cutter, the combine would lift the cutter up and off the trailer that I had been pulling with the pickup truck. Once the cutter had been raised high enough above the trailer, I would drive the pickup forward to clear the cutter from the trailer. From start to finish, we were there for about three hours to unload and set up the equipment for the farmer.

The entire time we were unloading and setting up the combine, the hardscrabble farmer who bought the combine was picking rocks out of his field and putting them in the bed of his pickup truck. I estimate each rock weighed between one and three pounds; they weren't small rocks.

As I watched the farmer picking rocks up and looking over the acreage he farmed, I could not help but wonder what the point was. There was a big field with a whole lot of rocks in the field.

His field went as far as the eye could see, and I can't imagine he could ever finish picking rocks from it. Even if he had been able to pick all the rocks from the field, my uncle Mike told me that the winter freeze would push new rocks to the surface. Once the spring thaw came around, there would be more new rocks to pick up.

I will always remember watching that farmer picking a never-ending supply of rocks from the field. A farmer's work is never finished.

The next summer, at seventeen, I drove to Montana, and from there I drove even further to visit my friend Mark. Mark was living with his uncle on a dairy farm in Lynden, Washington. Mark lived in Great Falls and was visiting and working for his uncle for the summer.

Mark's uncle ran a dairy farm, and Mark's summer job at the farm was to milk the cows. Milking the cows entails waking up early in the morning for the first milking and then milking them again in the early evening. Cows have to be milked twice a day, twelve hours apart, every day. In between milking the cows, Mark was the general farm hand, helping his uncle with the chores.

While we were there, a neighbor who was a gentleman farmer needed help baling hay and reached out to see if we could help. He was paying five bucks an hour cash, and as Mark and I were both in the business of making money, we accepted the offer.

It only took me one day of baling hay to realize I never wanted to do that again. After eight hours of lifting and throwing hay bales, my arms felt like jelly and my fingers were raw from slipping them under the strings holding the bales together. Let me explain the process.

Baling the hay occurs after the hay has been cut, left to dry in the field, and then assembled into bales. Once the hay has been assembled into bales, it is left in the field for another week or two. Leaving the hay in the field to dry out after each step reduces the moisture in the hay, making it easier to handle. I also think it has to be dry to store in the barn, but I'm not positive about that.

Collecting the hay, or as it's called, baling hay, has two main components. First, there are the guys who walk next to the flatbed trailer being pulled by the tractor. These guys grab the hay bales from the field and then toss the hay bales onto the trailer. The second part of baling the hay are the guys on the trailer who then stack the hay bales neatly and interlock them so they don't fall off the trailer during transport. The guys on the trailer are more experienced, as they know how to interlock the stacks so the trailer may travel without any hay bales falling off.

There is also a third part to baling hay; however, I didn't see this part, as I was in the field. The third part entails unloading the hay from the trailer onto a conveyer belt. The conveyer belt takes the hay to the second floor of the barn, where it is then stacked and stored for the winter.

The flatbed trailers that the hay is loaded onto are around eight feet wide and twenty feet long. The hay bales are loaded onto the trailer and are stacked six or seven bales high on the trailer. When done, the trailer full of hay bales make a perfect rectangle.

The last few bales of hay loaded onto the trailer are the bales that make the perfect rectangle. Of course, the last few bales are the also hardest to lift, as they have to be thrown over your head on top of the already stacked hay bales. The stacking crew on the trailer would catch the hay bale as it was thrown to them and then direct the hay bale to its place in the rectangle. The stacking crew on the trailer were so good, they caught and then stacked the hay bales in one smooth motion.

Once the trailer has been completely loaded, the hay bales are high and tightly packed. I didn't ask why they had to have a such a high and full trailer because I didn't want to sound like a spoiled suburban kid. I silently wondered why they couldn't just drive off before it became so hard to load them.

We didn't take many breaks either; the one break I recall was for lunch. During the hay baling operation, there were two trailers to be loaded. As there were two trailers, there was always an empty trailer at the ready to be loaded. The only people in this operation who had it easy were the drivers of the tractors.

The experienced members of the crew had given me some friendly advice before starting the day. They warned me to be careful and watch to make sure there weren't any rattlesnakes under the hay bales. Apparently, rattlesnakes like to live under the bales of hay. I look back and still have an appreciation for the warning to watch for rattlesnakes. I remember the warning, but I don't recall them telling me what to do if I actually discovered a snake. They were real helpful guys, and I suppose you just jump away when you hear the rattle.

The Career Lesson: Be it growing crops and picking rocks from never-ending fields on the northern edge of the country, milking cows twice a day, or baling hay until your arms feel like jelly, farming is some of the hardest work anywhere. When I'm having a hard day, I remind myself it isn't as hard as those days. Thank you, farmers!

Bonus Lesson: watch out for rattlesnakes under the bales of hay.

4
The Mall Experience

My first job out of school was a direct benefit of a friendship. Steve, my friend, was doing really well at the store/pharmacy at the Woodfield Mall in Schaumburg, Illinois. In fact, Steve was doing so well, he was a manager trainee. As a manager trainee, Steve had ascended as high as one can ascend in an hourly position before transitioning into a salaried assistant store manager role. As a manager trainee, Steve was qualified to carry the store keys. Carrying keys was a big deal, and Steve told me about how big a responsibility it was to carry the keys, several times over!

One of the benefits for Steve was that the managers modulated his hours by the fact that they would not allow him to incur excessive overtime pay. If Steve had transitioned to an assistant manager role, his hours would have gone up, and although his salary would have been greater, it would not have paced with the extra hours he would have to work. That's an okay trade-off if a management position at a store/pharmacy is your lifelong goal.

As I had spent the summer in Montana and Washington state visiting friends and family and fishing and hiking all over, I didn't have anything going on when I returned home. I look back and wonder why I even returned; I was having a grand time in Montana.

Being the good friend Steve is, he offered to help me get a job with him. Steve seemed to be doing well, so I accepted his offer. I bought a tie, and upon my first day on the job, I was awarded my own new-to-me blue smock!

Overall, the work was easy: stock shelves, run a cash register and do the random clean up in aisle three. On special occasions, I was able to use the cardboard baler too. Until I started watching "The Office" and saw that the office staff in Scranton weren't allowed to use the baler, I never really understood how special it was to be able to do that! The pay here was appropriate for the work, not great, but truthfully, I wasn't doing anything too great to earn better.

As I mentioned, the store we worked at was located in the Woodfield Mall in Schaumburg, Illinois. At the time, Woodfield was the largest mall in the world. The mall had to modify their claim to being the largest mall in the world of dedicated retail space once the Mall of America opened in Minnesota. I think there are even larger malls around the world now. It is easy to say that back in the day, the Woodfield Mall was an awesome place.

The best benefit to working in the Woodfield Mall was that I was a young single guy. Like all malls, Woodfield attracted a lot of young single girls shopping there. Even though I was in the store working, I was kind of shopping too. Looking back, I can't think of a better place for a young single guy to have worked at.

There were two managers above Steve: the manager, Gary, and the assistant manager, Steve. Gary, the manager took Steve aside one day and mentioned he was pleased with Steve's recommendation to hire me. Gary mentioned he had observed that I did the job well, except, as he told Steve, that I spent too much time helping the young women.

The manager shared that one of his observations was that I was helping young women even when they weren't seeking help. The manager explained to Steve that I needed to focus on the task at hand and not on trying to hold anyone's hand. As Steve brought me in, it was up to Steve to address my generous hospitality and put me back on track.

Steve took me aside and mentioned what the manager had told him about me. Steve was a young single guy too, so he may not have seen the problem in what I had been doing. Steve, being a good employee, followed through on the manager's request and spoke to me. I straightened up and focused on the job, mostly, most of the time. I owed it to Steve to do a good job and be a bit more discreet in my shopping.

Steve and I didn't last too much longer at the store. It was a great place to work, but there were better opportunities for the both of us.

The Career Lesson: Keep your eye on the job, not the girls.

Steve's Career Lesson: When you bring someone in, that someone will be your responsibility.

5
The River Rat

For the next step in my career, I became a carpenter. My father was a carpenter, and he felt it was time for me to get serious about life, and since I wasn't doing it on my own, he helped me along. I was now working with—and many times for—my father.

Early in my career, a good friend of my father's put me to task. The River Rat took it upon himself to test me by working me as hard as he could. He stated at the beginning of my first week with him that his intentions were to work me to the ground, and he kept to his word. Testing the new guy on the crew is common, and I was the new guy.

I wasn't afforded any special breaks, either, given that I was my father's son. Receiving special breaks would not have looked good for either of us. Looking back, I wonder if my father was an accomplice of the River Rat's and his intentions to break me. Either way, the River Rat kept his word and worked me hard with every intent of breaking me.

In the trade show world, the finishing touch before a show opens is the installation of the aisle carpet. The night before a show opens, the exhibitors complete their exhibit installation, and they exit the exhibit hall leaving the aisles filled with empty crates and trash. When they return the next morning, the aisles have been cleaned and aisle carpet has been installed. With the aisle carpet installed, the show floor looks like the showroom it is supposed to look like. When the aisle carpet is completed, the show is ready to open.

If I were given a dollar every time I heard an exhibitor, while walking into the exhibit hall on opening morning, say they didn't think the show would be ready to open when they walked out the night before—I would have a lot of dollars. It's easy to understand their skepticism while judging the condition of the aisles when they had left the previous evening. I am still impressed with the transition from littered and jammed aisles to being show ready, even considering all of the shows I have worked.

The actual task of installing the aisle carpet is a physically difficult task. Compounding the difficulty of the task is the fact that the typical installation time for aisle carpet is when normal humans are sleeping in their beds.

To give you an example of an aisle carpet challenge, in some cases the carpet is wider than the aisle, making a difficult task even more difficult. When the carpet is wider than the aisle, there is a lot of manhandling of the carpet so the exhibits and the product in the booths aren't damaged. The rolling out of the aisle carpet for show open and the rolling up of the aisle carpet upon show close are not fun or easy tasks.

As was common back in the day, the aisle carpet we were installing had been purchased, then installed, and upon being rolled up, it was then stored for each particular show. This carpet had been stored in a trailer for almost a year since the previous year's event. As the carpet was stacked in a trailer, the carpet rolls on the bottom of the stacks weren't round anymore; the rolls had become flat on two sides from the weight of the carpets on top of them. The rolls of carpet at the bottom of the pile were the flattest, and we called these flat carpet rolls "pancakes."

To install the pancake carpet rolls, you had to roll them out first by lifting them with your hands to advance the roll. Each time the carpet rolled over, there was a big thump as the other flat side hit the floor. Rolling out the carpet with your hands lasted until enough carpet had been unrolled and the carpet rolls could easily roll out by pushing it with your feet. In fact, as I write this, I can feel the dirt on my hands and arms from lifting the carpet rolls, and I can smell the mustiness of the carpet.

To make it even more difficult, back then the most durable carpet had a rubber backing. The rubber backing made it extremely heavy to move and roll out. As one can imagine, the task of installing this carpet was hard and boring.

Back to my experience with the River Rat. It was the night before show opening, and as the aisles were cleared of trash and empty crates, we were rolling out the carpet. True to his word, the River Rat did his best to work me to the ground. We rolled out a lot of aisle carpet that night, and it wore me out. I give the River Rat credit, because he almost succeeded in breaking me. The only reasons I was still standing after that night were my youth and not wanting to disappoint my father.

One day I almost extracted a little payback on the River Rat. We were on break, and there weren't any clean tables in the café, so I sat down at the cleanest dirty table. Next to me was a half-eaten breakfast that included a completely uneaten sausage patty.

Upon the River Rat's arrival to the table, he sat down and must have felt a need to exert his dominance by eating my breakfast, and he picked up the uneaten sausage patty, not knowing it wasn't mine. As he smiled and began bragging how he was going to eat the sausage from my plate, I must have broken enough of a smile to give him some warning. The River Rat asked if it was indeed my plate, and I replied by asking if it mattered. I'm sorry to say he put the sausage back on the plate, and then he smiled too.

The Career Lesson: Someone will test you on the job, and you will find the strength and determination to pass the test.

The second Career Lesson: Work on your poker face; you never know when you'll need it.

6
Everyone Gets One Pass

In my early days working the show floor, I wasn't well known and I didn't work for all of the various contractors. When a contractor was in the facility that I didn't have a connection with, there was still a way to seek work and be hired on with them. Gaining work with the other contractors was possible by sitting in the labor pool. Please let me explain.

Typically, a foreman would call in the crew size he felt were needed to do the job for the day. These people were typically his regular crew. However, on some days, there would be unanticipated additional work, and additional crews were needed.

As the work load was greater, the foreman would need to hire on more people to complete the work. As this was a typical occurrence, the foreman would go into the labor pool and hire the additional people he needed to complete the day's work.

The labor pool was a place where carpenters were able to take a chance to be hired just by showing up and waiting for work.

With the possibility of gaining work just by showing up by sitting in the labor pool, there was always the possibility to be hired on. On the other side of the coin, there were many times when there wasn't additional work and the day was wasted sitting in the pool without working.

Going to sit in the labor pool for a chance to work was also a good way to show your enthusiasm to work. Sitting in the labor pool was also a way of paying your dues, especially for a new guy. After a while, if you were a good worker and had proven yourself, you would move up in the ranks and be hired more often by having been present and ready to work. For me, there were many times when the foreman would come up to me and say there was not work that day, but show up tomorrow and I would be put to work then.

On one particular event, I went to McCormick Place to take a chance to get hired and sat in the labor pool. The event moving in served the steel mill industry. I recall I was there the second day of move in and there were flatbed tractor trailers inside the exhibit hall with large pieces of foundry equipment on the flatbed trailers.

The foundry pieces to be unloaded that day were rather large, and unloading them required the use of forklifts and cranes. As the exhibit floor was full of trucks, forklifts, and cranes, there wasn't much else going on that day because of the space needed to be able maneuver all of the equipment.

After seeing what was going on that morning, I didn't think there would be work for me that day. My plan shifted to hanging around for a couple hours to make sure the foreman saw me and leaving after traffic had settled down. I didn't want to leave too early, as the morning rush hour was still in progress. Typically, on my way to work, I would leave early in the morning to avoid the traffic, and I wasn't thrilled to be in the middle of morning traffic on the way home.

While I was waiting for the right time to leave, and much to my surprise, the foreman called me and assigned me to work with an exhibitor to construct his booth. The booth was on the forty-two level on the west wall. I am still not able to figure out the timing on this. The exhibit I was assigned to build was a small ten-foot inline booth on the perimeter of the massive exhibit hall.

I was puzzled as to why this exhibitor was in a hurry to set up his inline booth when all of the equipment was active on the floor. There were also quite a few days before the show opened, so there was no reason he shouldn't have waited to build his booth. The foreman signed me in and sent me to the booth. Seems all the hanging around to be noticed was starting to pay off.

Upon arriving to the booth, I started constructing the frame and discovered there was a cloth banner that snapped onto the frame. In most convention cities, this wouldn't be a problem, but it used to be included in another union's jurisdiction in Chicago. As carpenters, we built exhibits—*except* when there were cloth or staples involved in the exhibit.

The decorators' union claimed the work I was doing. I knew constructing the booth was the jurisdiction of the decorators. I took the chance of finishing the construction of the booth under the radar without being discovered. I wanted to complete the installation and at least earn the hour of pay that would be enough to cover my parking cost for the day.

As I was finishing the booth build, thinking I was going to finish without getting caught doing the decorators' work, the decorator steward drove up on his scooter. He informed me that I was not supposed to be building that exhibit. It was his union's jurisdiction.

I was still a young man and not well enough known, so I was able to act as if I didn't know the rules. The decorator steward was rather direct as he informed me that I was crossing the jurisdiction lines; however, he was also very respectful about it. He instructed me to dismantle the booth so his members could reconstruct it and thus protect their work jurisdiction.

I look back and wonder about the steward. He knew that as a carpenter, my working in that booth may be the only hour I worked for the day. I know he knew that, and I wonder if he waited long enough for me to realize that one hour of pay before he went to the booth to stop me. I didn't think about that at the time; had I thought about it I would have thanked him.

As he instructed, I dismantled the exhibit and then signed out of that labor ticket. I received my hour of pay for that one job.

Going forward, I knew I would not get away with doing decorator work again. The next time, the decorator steward would recognize me and the toll I would pay would be a lot higher, and I didn't want to deal with that. To this day, I still appreciate how the decorator steward was a gentleman as he was sharing the work rules with me.

The Career Lesson: You can only act as if you don't know the rules once; the first time is the only time. After that, if you choose to break the rules, be ready for the consequences.

7
Good Time Charlie

As a newer carpenter, I was learning something new all the time. In the trade show industry there are a lot of unique job tasks most people wouldn't associate with the stereotypical carpentry tasks such as building a house. This was especially true when a machinery show would be in town.

Good Time Charlie was an older man who was always hanging around the labor pool. He certainly looked the part of being a good carpenter; he always wore matching Carhartt pants, shirts, jacket, and hat. Even though Good Time Charlie was always around, he worked infrequently. It may have been because he came across as a sour old guy and always had a smart aleck remark at the ready.

I recall a couple of his standard remarks, however; they weren't appropriate then and they're certainly not appropriate now. I never knew his real name either; everyone knew him as "Good Time Charlie," and that is what he answered to.

One day Good Time Charlie and I were partnered together to work in a booth as millwrights. Millwrights assemble machinery, and in McCormick Place the carpenters are the millwrights. In most cases, when working as millwrights, as in this case as well, we were working with a crew of riggers.

The riggers operate the forklifts to lift and move the machinery into place, enabling the millwrights to bolt the assemblies together. Once the assemblies were completed, we had built working conveyers and assembly lines right on the show floor.

Joe Pestka

The day was going along fine, with Good Time Charlie and me keeping busy assembling the machinery as the riggers set the pieces in place. During this process, I learned that a drift pin is an invaluable tool for doing this job effectively.

A typical drift pin used while assembling machinery is a one-foot-long hardened steel rod that is tapered on one end from about a quarter-inch thick ascending to one inch thick in the span of eight inches of the pin. The last section of the drift pin is about four inches, and it is not tapered, as this part forms the handle. There are larger drift pins used for larger machinery; however, we did not need anything that big for this application.

The utility of the drift pin is that it allows a millwright to align two elements of a machine for assembly. As each new element of the machine is added to the already assembled machinery, the bolt holes are guided to match up to each other with the use of the drift pin.

The process to match up two pieces of machinery includes the drift pin first being inserted into the bolt hole of the stationary piece of machinery with the narrow end of the drift pin ready to receive and align the new piece of machinery. Then, as the new piece of machinery nears the stationary piece of equipment, the narrow end of the drift pin is inserted into the bolt hole of the new piece of machinery, thus guiding it into place to be able to then bolt the pieces together.

Once the two pieces of machinery are aligned with the use the drift pin, one is now able to bolt the two pieces of the machinery together.

Given that this was my first time working as a millwright, I wasn't aware of the existence of, or of my needing, a drift pin. Good Time Charlie was an old timer and had a drift pin. He was almost able to maintain pace with the riggers by himself; however, with my not having my own drift pin, he was not able to carry me and keep up.

Toward the end of the day the riggers and Good Time Charlie gave me some grief for not having my own drift pin, as I was slowing down the operation. I think it may have been close to quitting time, and we were working in a section of the exhibit hall that was exposed to the sun without any breeze, and it was hot, so it had been a long day.

Good Time Charlie, never missing an opportunity to disperse his sourness, piled the grief on me. Good Time Charlie wanted to know what kind of millwright I was as I didn't have a drift pin of my own. Being under pressure, the only reply I could come up with was that the crews I usually worked with were able to set the machinery in place just fine without my needing a drift pin, so I never bothered to get one!

The riggers and Good Time Charlie had a good laugh. The riggers I was working with that day were good guys, as they gave me a second break for the day. The first break was for not having the right tools, and the second break was for my being a smart aleck. I may also have gotten a break as they may have known my father. Whatever the reason, they gave me an unearned pass.

After that day, I did go out and buy a drift pin; however, I never needed to use it. As I had moved up in the ranks, my job assignments didn't include being a millwright, so I stopped carrying the drift pin in my tool bag.

The Career Lesson: Have the right tool for the job and always have a comeback remark at the ready, but keep it to yourself.

Second Career Lesson: If you ever work with a guy with a name like "Good Time Charlie," you should expect an unusual day.

8
Shuffle Along Stanley

Shuffle Along Stanley was one of the older men that came to the labor pool every day but rarely worked. As the name implies, Shuffle Along Stanley didn't really walk in a typical manner; he shuffled his feet to get where he was going. When he shuffled along, he didn't even make a full step. Each time he shuffled, he only moved about the length of his other foot. He was very slow moving.

As one can imagine, because of his slow gait, Shuffle Along Stanley didn't work very often. If he worked at all, it was only when he was the last person available in the labor pool. His rate of production was what one would expect for a guy who shuffled along. His English was not too good either, so communicating with him was difficult.

Usually, at some point in the day, Shuffle Along Stanley would become fed up with not working. This is when he would blow a whistle as loudly as he could in the labor pool to gain attention. This proved to be annoying, but was never effective, as he didn't gain any additional work from his attention grab.

The story I heard was that when Shuffle Along Stanley was a young man, he worked the oil fields in the Middle East, where he made a ton of money. This was hard work and took an obvious toll on his body, particularly his feet. As he was working outside the United States, he didn't earn any retirement credits. Although he made great money, seems he didn't save any of it.

The story includes his spending his money on wine, women, and song. Now, with the oil field work done and having spent all his money, Shuffle

Along Stanley was in a difficult position. He found himself sitting in the labor pool looking for a few hours to get by on.

I don't recall noticing when Shuffle Along Stanley stopped coming around, and nobody mentioned anything about it either. He just faded out of the picture and wasn't there anymore. Sometimes I look back and still feel sad for the guy.

> **The Career Lesson:** Protect your health and finances, and plan, especially for retirement. Wine, women, and song are a lot of fun; however, there is always a tomorrow, so save some money for it.

9
PJ

PJ was another of the older man who spent most of his time in the labor pool. PJ did not gain a lot of work, but he was always there with a smile and a good outlook on life.

Looking back, I realize there may have been a few reasons the older men were always in the labor pool. In a carpenter's retirement, there was a provision that allowed one to work a few hours each month without impact to one's retirement benefits. These older men may have been seeking a few extra bucks to supplement their pension.

The money may have been important; however, I think the primary reason they all showed up ready for work was out of the habit of having gone to work their entire lives. After a lifetime of going to work, it may have been a difficult habit to break for these men.

The third reason they may have all showed up for work, and maybe the most important for some of them, was that it allowed them to maintain a social life with their friends. Once the workday had started at 8:00 a.m., if they were not working, they all migrated to their little circles of friends and began playing cards or just talking it up over coffee.

Back to PJ. He was a rather sociable guy; he greeted everyone with a smile and a "good morning" or a "how are you doing." I always thought PJ should have been somewhere else grandfathering, as he seemed like such a nice person.

After sitting in the labor pool all day, the older men would start to depart around two thirty in the afternoon. PJ would leave and his go-to parting phrase was always "Better days ahead, boys." The other older men would purse their lips and nod their heads in agreement. There wasn't a lot of conversation at this point, as their disappointment from not working had dimmed their enthusiasm.

Doing the math in my head, with this being the early eighties and considering PJ was in his late sixties or early seventies, I figured his statement of "better days ahead" was a reference to being around during the Great Depression. Economically times were tough in the early eighties too, although not depression tough. The early eighties had high interest rates, high inflation, and high unemployment rates, a triple play. As bad as the eighties were, PJ and the other men in the labor pool had lived through much worse in their lives.

The Career Lesson: When times are tough, there are better days ahead. When times are good, save some money, as nothing lasts forever.

10
Slim Felice

When I first started working in the trade show industry, there were still quite a few men who had started their careers much earlier when a significant portion of their time was spent producing trade shows in hotels. Trade shows in the hotels usually had exhibits in the ballroom and in the hotel rooms. The hotel rooms had the bed and other furniture removed and were then able to be used as exhibition space. The hotel rooms created an effective showroom, particularly effective for showing products privately.

Back in the day, the experience of working in a hotel included a lot of tipping, and tipping became seamless for an exhibitor. Upon arrival at the hotel, the exhibitor had the door opened by the doorman, whom they tipped. After checking in, the bellman delivered their luggage to their room, and the Bellman was tipped. They ate at the café and tipped the server. There was a tip for housekeeping too. As show labor helped the exhibitor set up their booth, they were also tipped. As it had been explained to me, everyone was tipped back then.

As the events began to grow to be too large for the hotels, and dedicated convention centers became more common, trade shows migrated to the convention centers. The convention centers were able to accommodate the growth of the events and placed everyone in a common exhibit hall. As trade shows migrated from the hotels to dedicated convention centers, the practice of exhibitors giving everybody a tip was left behind in the hotels as well.

This is where Slim Felice comes into the story. Slim Felice left the hotels with everyone else, but he didn't leave his attachment for the tips there.

Although I didn't work with Slim Felice very often, I can say that when I did, it was always lucrative. Slim Felice wasn't afraid to ask for a tip, and to his credit, he was generous in splitting it with his silent partner. On a few of the days that I worked with Slim Felice, I made as much in tips as I earned in wages. As a bonus, on top of getting a tip, the tips were in cash!

The setup Slim Felice used to ask for a tip was pretty simple. While providing a service the exhibitor had already paid for, Slim Felice would expound on how it was his one and only goal to make sure we did a great job for them and that they were happy. He would make the task look as difficult as possible while working up a sweat and telling the exhibitor how hard we were working for him the entire time. Upon completion, the exhibitor felt they were obligated to say thank you, and many times they willingly provided a tip.

When there was only a verbal thank you from the exhibitor, Slim Felice would introduce a few sly tactics to have the exhibitor cough up the cash tip. The sly tactics were not over the top, but the intentions of extracting gratuity were clear. My favorite tactic was this: if you weren't aware—as many of the exhibitors weren't until Slim Felice told them—"you can't buy milk for the babies with a thank you." It was simple but effective.

Believe me when I say I loved the cash tips, but it was also uncomfortable. This was common in the early days, and it was questionable in the early eighties. I couldn't imagine it happening today.

The Career Lesson: Give an honest day's work for an honest day's pay, deliver the services the client requested and paid for with a smile. They are keeping you employed.

11
The Carpet Crew

There used to be a general contractor based a little further east from Chicago, and they produced several large shows in McCormick Place. In Chicago, this general contractor had a small staff in a small warehouse with a small production crew. The office was large enough to produce hotel shows, just not large enough for the McCormick Place shows. When they did have a large show in town, they brought staff in and used local labor as supervisors. When they were in town with a big show, I hired on to one of their carpet crews.

The carpet crew was a great place to be, as I would be hired first and kept on until the move-out was completed. The reason for being there from start to finish of the event is that the installation of the booth carpet must occur before exhibits are constructed. Then, after the event had concluded and after everything has been dismantled and taken from off of the carpet, it must be rolled up to be loaded out.

There were benefits realized as an hourly paid person working for a contractor that didn't have a full service operation in the city. As an out of town general contractor, they usually had a few logistical challenges with the trucking of materials being delayed or missing pieces, which usually resulted in additional hours for the crew to complete jobs. There were other things that affected their efficiency too; let me explain that with a little more detail.

There were a few guys on the carpet crew that didn't return to work after lunch as productive as when they left for lunch. They were most likely with the foreman, and all were having a great time. I look back and realize that it was a good thing they weren't as productive after lunch.

The advantage I realized from members of the crew not returning with the same productivity after lunch was that the foreman had to factor in the lack of productivity in their labor calls. The lack of productivity meant they had to increase their labor calls. The advantage for me was that I was part of the factor for getting the work done.

When lunch concluded, I returned from lunch and was still very productive. Along with the other guys that returned from lunch the same, we became an important part of the crew, as we kept things moving along at show site in the afternoon. If the after-lunch crew had been able to put in an honest full day of work, I most likely wouldn't have been needed and wouldn't have worked the show.

I was not upset for having to carry the additional weight after lunch. I knew the reason I had been hired on was to cover for the members of the crew who realized a drop in their productivity. I smiled all the way to the bank.

The Career Lesson: Sometimes you shouldn't worry about what others are doing—or not doing. You can only control what you do, and that's all that counts.

12
The Pare

The Pare and I were partners while working three trade shows every year. The shows were back to back, and as partners, we worked together quite a lot in a short amount of time. The time we spent together amounted to about 35 days or 280 hours annually.

While working with a partner for that long of a time, you develop a bond with each other. As the junior member of our partnership, I did more of the listening than talking. The Pare provided a ton of funny stories, many of his stories were from his early days working in the industry.

I still recall a couple of the Pare's stories. The first story is about one of his previous partners from his early days in the business, who liked to take a nap after lunch upon his return to the job. The Pare shared that this guy napped as he was sleeping off mostly what he had drunk during lunch, maybe a little of what he had eaten too.

To maximize his comfort during naptime, the guy would take his shoes off. How quaint: return to work after lunch and take a nap while getting paid for it! The difficult part for this guy was that while he was happily napping, his coworkers would take and hide his shoes. It sounds like they may have been a little perturbed that he was napping and they weren't.

Not having his shoes made for a difficult afternoon for the guy. He would go looking for his shoes while walking in his socks in the middle of a convention center. I always wondered why this guy didn't learn his lesson after the first few times it happened and just keep his shoes on while napping.

The other interesting bit of information the Pare shared while we worked together was the location in the exhibit hall where he had hidden his pint of whatever he used to drink. If you can imagine, an exhibit hall is pretty wide open, and there aren't many nooks or crannies available. It was mostly concrete and columns.

As barren as an exhibit hall is, one has to be very creative to be able to hide a pint. As the Pare had been on the wagon for several years, he was able to share his hiding locations with me without concern. Upon learning of all of his hiding spots, I realized I had a new-found appreciation for his creativity.

The Pare was a busy guy too. He wasn't busy about getting things done; he was really busy just trying to look busy, all the while doing as little as possible. He put more effort into looking busy than if he had just been busy completing the task at hand and then moving on to the next task. We had plenty of work on the three shows we were together, so we didn't need to slow down to preserve our place on the crew.

As I mentioned, the Pare had been in the business for a while, so he still had some old habits. Lucky for the Pare, he also had some relatives in the business and was able to game the system based on his connections.

The Career Lesson: It is much easier to be busy and to accomplish tasks than it is to just look busy doing nothing. Give an honest day's work for a day's pay. If you do need a nap, keep your shoes on!

13
The Dodger

In my early days, I worked a few shifts with the Dodger. Although the Dodger and I didn't work together often, the times I did work with him were always an interesting time. The Dodger wasn't your stereotypical labor guy. He stood about five feet five inches tall, and he was almost as round as he was tall.

The Dodger started each day with a cigar worthy of Winston Churchill. By the end of day, the cigar was just long enough to extend past his lips. The only time he didn't have the cigar in his mouth was when he was eating.

When we were partners, he did a lot of instructing and encouraging, and I did most of the doing. As one might imagine the Dodger didn't have a great deal of mobility, so he took the lead as supervisor, leaving me to do the work. Looking back, I suppose his guidance was good training and his encouraging words were good for my self-esteem.

The Dodger didn't work a lot of hours, and yet he drove a nice, late model Cadillac. I recall that the Cadillac had the impressive, solid whitewall tires that were popular at the time, along with open shirt collars and gold chains. In the beginning, I wasn't sure how the Dodger's economics panned out, considering he drove a nice car yet the hours he worked weren't that great.

During a conversation, the Dodger shared that he was the last person one would meet when they owed the wrong people money. As I was from the suburbs, I wasn't up on the terms for street loans. The Dodger elaborated and told me the money he collected was for delinquent juice loans and gambling debts.

I was able to connect the dots to this line of work thanks to Rocky Balboa. If you have seen the movie *Rocky*, you may recall that Rocky is a boxer and a juice loan collector. In the beginning of the movie, Rocky is instructed by his boss to collect some money, and if the guy doesn't pay, Rocky is supposed to break his fingers. Rocky is too good natured to beak the guy's fingers. The matter-of-fact delivery by the Dodger as he was sharing what he did led me to believe he wouldn't have had any problem breaking fingers.

This also explained the Dodger's economics and his ability to drive a nice Cadillac.

At the time, I wondered—and I still wonder—how the Dodger could be successful if he needed to chase someone to collect money. As I already mentioned, he didn't move fast at work. The Dodger was smart; he probably caught up with people when they least expected it.

I have since read that street loans aren't really a thing anymore, as credit cards have replaced them. Think about that while you're racking up your credit cards. Credit cards are the legal juice loans of today. On the positive side, if you're late or miss a payment on your credit card, they might ding your credit rating, but your fingers won't be broken and you don't need to look over your shoulder.

One day, while on a break and having coffee together, the Dodger offered me an opportunity in a limited partnership. The Dodger explained that he was too well known with the local authorities, so he was in need of an unknown partner to capitalize on this opportunity. The Dodger needed someone the authorities didn't know of, like me.

The Dodger then explained that my being from the suburbs, with a clean rap sheet, made me the perfect candidate for the opportunity. The Dodger went on to explain that my end of the partnership was simple. It would mostly be just the paperwork.

My role in our partnership would consist of buying and insuring properties in neighborhoods he knew were good for this type of endeavor. After I purchased and insured the properties, the Dodger would then burn them down. Once the building had been burned down to the ground and the smoke had cleared, I would collect the insurance money, and then we would split the surplus.

Career Lessons

After every job, our partnership would be put on the back burner (pun intended) until the coast had cleared, and then we would re-engage our partnership. The Dodger figured we could do this every couple of months on additional buildings in various wards in the city without the authorities catching on.

I thanked the Dodger for the opportunity and then respectfully declined. My rap sheet was clean as I did not have a rap sheet, and my rap sheet is still clean to this day. I never shared this partnership proposition with my father or anyone else at the time. I'm not sure why I didn't tell my father, maybe because the Dodger accepted my decline without any resistance. I have kept this opportunity to myself until now.

Another experience with the Dodger was during an exhibit installation that we were working twelve-hour shifts for seven days straight to complete for show opening. This exhibit had two levels that we built on a major show that used to occur every June in Chicago. As you can imagine, after a few days of working noon to midnight, everyone was getting a little worn down. Usually in these situations, the team drew a little closer, as we were all in the same boat and we shared a common goal.

There was a new guy on our crew this year. The new guy had just been released after time served and somehow found a place on our crew. The new guy also drove a nice, late model Cadillac with big whitewall tires.

I didn't get to know the new guy, as I was a little intimidated by him, so I steered clear of him. I don't recall his name either, and even if I could remember his name, I wouldn't use it here. For the purposes of referring to him in the book, I have assigned a name to him based on what I do remember the most about him.

What I found the most memorable about this guy was that he looked really tough. He had a shaved head, was muscular, and moved in stop-action-like movements, similar to the Cyclops in the original *Sinbad* movie. When he spoke, he mostly blurted statements, as he was not an articulate person. He didn't need to be articulate, as he had a way to always get his point across and he was very direct. From here on, I will refer to him as the Cyclops.

For an unknown reason, the Cyclops and the Dodger didn't get along, and they began to banter with each other. I found their bickering a little

43

perplexing, as they seemed similar in their backgrounds. I thought they should have gotten along really well, especially considering they most likely had similar back stories. They could have at least talked about Cadillacs and whitewall tires. As the week wore on their bickering became more competitive.

During a dinner break, the bantering became a little more animated and a lot more serious. After a few back and forth statements, the Cyclops stood up and loudly exclaimed that if he and the Dodger were stranded on a desert island and there was only one coconut, the Cyclops would eat it by himself. He bragged that the Dodger would starve.

The Dodger didn't stand up or stop eating his dinner. His calm and measured reply has stuck with me, as it was one of the best replies I have ever heard. The Dodger replied that if they indeed were stranded together on a desert island, he would first eat the cyclops for dinner, then have the coconut for dessert. He wasn't going to go hungry; in fact, he was going to be quite content.

The Cyclops was caught off guard by that statement, and he wasn't quick or smart enough to assemble a fitting reply. As tough as the Cyclops was, his debating capacity was mostly limited. I wonder if he went home and had coconut for dessert that night.

The rest of the shift went smoothly, as the natural order of tough guys must have been established. I don't recall ever seeing the Cyclops again, and as my role expanded, I wasn't working with the Dodger anymore either. I sometimes wonder what happened to the both of those guys.

The Career Lessons:
1. Don't borrow money or gamble with credit from these types of people.
2. Vet partnerships really well, especially partnerships that aren't "Limited Liability."
3. The toughest of the tough guys save their coconuts for dessert.

14
Scottie Boy

Scottie Boy and I were partners for quite a few years in our early days as carpenters. Scottie Boy gained his name with the rest of us, as we were nick-named Scottie Boy, Joey Boy, Sammy Boy, and Jimmy Boy. We were in Louisville, and one of our crew members was a fan of *The Waltons*, and our new names were a play on John Boy.

Scottie Boy was my neighbor while growing up, and he was a few years older than I was. He was a great partner, as he had real carpentry skills and, more importantly, was like a big brother. Having a partner who was a little older with more life experience and whom I trusted was a big benefit for me. I was still inexperienced and a bit of a smart aleck, so it was good to have a friend with me.

Scottie Boy and I had a lot of fun at work, and we had success gaming a few systems when an opportunity would present itself.

While the McCormick north building was under construction, we discovered we could park for free by telling the parking attendant we worked for one of the construction contractors.

Construction workers didn't have to pay to park; however, the show workers had to pay for parking. You never know what you might gain until you try.

We kept the ruse up as long as we could; it lasted for some of the time during the construction of the building and for a little while after construction was completed. One day the parking attendant was inside the building and saw us setting up a show. She came right up to us to tell us the jig was up. After that happened, we were back to paying for parking again.

After that, every time we saw the parking attendant in the parking booth, she had a big smile on her face. She was such a nice person, and she must have appreciated our creativity for the ruse, or she just liked us. Either way, she did not hold our ruse against us.

Scottie Boy was a good sport too. I played a few pranks on him, and I still use many of them on my kids when I can.

My favorite was passing by Scottie Boy and pushing my finger in Scottie Boy's back while at the same time pulling the trigger on the screw gun in my other hand. The first reaction is that someone thinks they are being drilled into. It's a little unsettling, to say the least.

We would also drive to work with my father in his Ford pickup. On the commute, driving in, I was in the middle of the bench seat, and on the way out, Scottie Boy sat in the middle. As we were pulling out of the parking lot to go home, I would reach down to tie my shoes. When I did this, it left Scottie Boy and my father next to each other in a cozy-looking situation. There were a few stares as we pulled out, and after they realized why they were receiving the odd stares, they made sure my shoes were tied before getting into the truck.

I'll say it again: Scottie Boy was a good sport.

There were many more fun times, but telling those stories isn't the intent of this book. This book is to share the Career Lessons and learning from them.

The Career Lesson: Having a trusted partner is one of the best things you can have while at work.

The second Career Lesson: we should have bought the parking attendant a box of chocolates or something nice for being such a good sport about our ruse.

15
Michael Me Lad

Michael primarily worked at one of the smaller facilities where we produced trade shows. The facility was not too busy, but there was enough work there to keep a couple guys busy for most of the year. Guys like me who kept busy at McCormick Place only cycled through this facility several times a year, when there were larger events going on.

Michael was an Irishman from the old country, and he spoke with a thick accent. He was hard to understand when he spoke, and many times I just smiled and shook my head in agreement as we spoke, pretending to know what he said. Michael was a naturally nice guy too; he always had a smile, and his friendly disposition was always pleasant to be around. It was also kind of neat to be called "lad" too.

Considering Michael's accent and a few other factors, he was darn near impossible to understand after lunch. It didn't matter too much after lunch anyway; once he made his appearance, we might not see him for the rest of the afternoon.

Many mornings we started with laying the aisle and booth carpet in the exhibit hall. As an elevator and conveyer belt served this hall, there usually wasn't a great amount of freight or forklift traffic; thus it allowed us to install all the carpet first. We would break up into crews of two or three, with Michael bouncing between crews helping to kick out the carpet.

When I say "kick out the carpet," I mean that we would push it with our feet to roll it out. First, when we started to roll the carpet out, we pushed the carpet using our heels with the roll behind us. Then as the carpet was a little lighter, we would turn and face the carpet, roll lifting and pushing it toe first.

Shoes didn't last long in this job, as the backing of carpet is a very rough surface, sort of like sand paper.

It's also worth mentioning that the carpet was used and reused in this hall without being sent out to be cleaned. The carpet had an accumulation of dirt and tacks in it, making it heavier than a typical carpet and occasionally quite painful for your knees when you found one of the tacks while seaming it together.

While rolling out the carpet, Michael always showed up in the middle of the roll and in his thick Irish accent would encouragingly state, "the more legs the lighter the load." Michael was right: the more legs the lighter the load while rolling out that carpet. Michael usually wasn't helping in the beginning of the roll when it was at its heaviest, but as nice as Michael was, we always appreciated his encouragement and his help.

When a larger event was in this facility, word got out, and there would be more workers showing up than there was work for everyone. In many cases, the men that showed up had paid to park and weren't going to work to earn money. This was in the early eighties before the economy was doing well. It was up to Michael to let the men know there wasn't going to be enough work to go around.

Michael would go out into the labor pool and visit with each man individually. Michael would tell each person that he was a good man but there wasn't enough work to go around. His closing message to each man was, "You're a good man; we just can't use you today." I suppose that may have been a common phrase from the Depression.

It was tough duty to let those men know there wasn't enough work for them, and Michael did it with kindness, respect, and empathy for each person.

The Career Lessons: Be kind when others are having a difficult day, and Michael was right: the more legs the lighter the load.

16
Queenie

Queenie was on our crew, and he was a older and polite gentleman. As the elder statesmen on our crew, he did not have to carry any tools or do any heavy work. Looking back, I don't think he really knew much about assembling booths or construction principles.

What Queenie lacked in output he made up in being a great motivator. Queenie kept everyone else working with encouraging comments. Nobody seemed to mind either; he was so likable he that didn't need to do any of the heavy lifting.

Queenie was an older man when I worked with him. He was about five feet three inches tall and always wore a hat, which was usually a driver's cap and occasionally a trilby hat (I had to look up the names of the hats). He typically dressed in matching powder blue pants and shirt sets like the ones you see in the Rat Pack movies from the sixties. Queenie was someone I always liked to be with; he had an aura that drew you in, and he was a person you couldn't help but like and respect.

I look back, and I don't recall if I ever knew Queenie's real name. While I worked with Queenie, I didn't know about his past career either. Much later, after Queenie had retired, I learned that when he was a young man, he had been a wheelman, or in today's term, a driver, for Al Capone. That explains the driver's hat!

I can only imagine the stories Queenie didn't tell me.

As Queenie had an aura that people respected, he helped to diffuse a situation that included an angry exhibitor. I wasn't there and don't recall if I ever knew why the exhibitor was upset. I do recall being told that the exhibitor was yelling at the service desk staff and they weren't able to calm him down. Upon Queenie's arrival, he took the exhibitor aside and spoke with him.

The conversation with Queenie calmed the exhibitor down, and things returned to normal. The move-out of the show was over, and upon turning in his bill of lading for his outbound shipment, the exhibitor left the show without additional incident.

My understanding of what happened after the exhibitor left the service desk goes something like this: obviously, as this happened a long time ago, I am not able to verify any of the details. Queenie provided a bit of payback to the exhibitor for his being rude to the staff, who did not deserve the grief they were given by the exhibitor.

Once the exhibitor had left the service desk, the story goes that Queenie changed the shipping destination of the outbound materials from New Jersey to California or from California to New Jersey. We were in Chicago, and the exhibitor's materials went to the opposite coast from where they were supposed to go.

Back in those days, there weren't any computers or the checks and balances that we have today. The power of the pen was still where the power resided. If the exhibitor was upset at the desk, I can only imagine how upset he was when he had to have his materials shipped back through Chicago from across the United States to the correct destination.

The Career Lesson: Queenie's actions illustrate that it's much easier and less costly to just be nice to people. Confrontation isn't effective, especially with the folks who are just doing their jobs on your behalf. You might make your point and win the argument you started, but you may still very well lose.

17
Tony the Head

Tony was another senior member of the crew I worked with. Tony wore his shirt unbuttoned at the top, with a lot of gold around his neck and on his chest. Tony said that people often mistakenly identified him as Burt Reynolds while out in public, as he had a mustache and the sly boyish grin to go with it.

I never stopped to ask how Tony earned his nickname. I suppose that is just what I knew him as when I met him, so I never thought anything about it.

Tony had the ability to lighten up every day at work, especially on the long days. He would do things like start singing "Over There" from the song the doughboys of World War I sang, or he would start repeating one-liners from Al Pacino and Robert Di Niro movies so many times that it eventually became funny and you were saying it too.

"What are you looking at?"

After a while, everyone was singing with Tony or repeating the same movie lines he had started saying.

One early Sunday morning, we were setting up a private product event at a downtown Chicago Hotel. Tony and I ran out to get coffee for the crew. We had started early that morning, and just before 7:00 a.m., it was almost break time, so we ran out while the rest of the crew was still working in the ballroom.

Upon our return, we had reached the facility dock, where a homeless man came up and asked us for money for food. By the looks of the man,

I was pretty sure that if we gave him money, he was not going to buy any food. Tony reached in his pocket and gave the homeless man five dollars anyway. As Tony was handing him the money, he embraced the man's hands with his hands and asked the man to promise to buy food. The man promised profusely.

After the man had departed, Tony looked at me and said he knew the man wasn't going to buy food. Tony said he wanted to help him out anyway. Tony had a big heart behind all that big gold.

The Career Lesson: Keep work fun and the time does go by quicker.

The Human Lesson: it's okay to be nice to someone who is down and to give them something in the hope they do the right thing, even when they most likely won't.

By the way, what are you looking at?

18
Skeeter Bomb!

I don't know how in the world one earns the nickname Skeeter Bomb, but that was his nickname.

I didn't know Skeeter Bomb as well as the other men. Frankly, Skeeter Bomb didn't like me, and we rarely spoke. He mostly sneered at me as we passed each other. Even though Skeeter Bomb didn't like me and we didn't speak often, he still provided a great example for a young man.

Skeeter Bomb was one of the hardest workers I knew. He started his career as a young man working in concrete. As I have helped on a few concrete jobs, I believe it has to be one of the hardest and most physically demanding ways to make a living. Everything about concrete is heavy, and as a result, everyone in the concrete business is very strong. I suppose the concrete work was so hard that it made the work we were doing in a convention center seem easy in comparison.

During one of the brief periods of time we were on speaking terms, Skeeter Bomb told me about the concrete business he had owned. He told me his concrete business was growing fast and was going great, so great that he had to expand.

He had bought ten brand new dump trucks to be able to handle all of the work he had. Then one morning he went to his yard and found all of his new dump trucks were missing, as they had been stolen overnight. He collected his insurance money but didn't want to be in the business anymore. Something about this seemed familiar.

Once out of the concrete business, Skeeter Bomb entered the trade show business. Even though we usually were not on good terms, I respected

Skeeter Bomb and his ability to ramrod and complete a task no matter the circumstances. If he had a task to do, he was getting it done—no matter what. Many times Skeeter Bomb completed his task without regard for the impact it had on other elements of the event production.

Sometimes, when completing his task, it negatively affected another element of the move-in and resulted in someone else taking longer to complete their tasks. Skeeter Bomb completed his objectives; however, he had made someone else's tasks more difficult. None of this mattered to Skeeter Bomb; all he wanted to do was to check his box completed.

Today the concept of improving efficiency and getting things done is studied and analyzed and then new processes are implemented. There are smart people who make a living telling other smart people how to do things more efficiently.

Skeeter Bomb was smart, although he didn't have a name for what he did, but he made a living getting it done faster and better. Skeeter Bomb always got the job done, and today he may have been able to make a living telling other people how to do it faster and better.

The Career Lesson: Sometimes getting it done efficiently is as simple as just leaning in and getting it done.

The second Career Lesson: Mentors aren't always obvious; you can learn from watching people who aren't taking you under their wing.

The third Career Lesson: Almost anything is easier to do than concrete work.

19
Rudy

When Rudy was a young man, he entered the workforce as a bricklayer. Years later, when I met Rudy, he was making his living as a carpenter. While a young man, Rudy had followed in his father's footsteps into the brick laying trade.

When we worked together, Rudy would share stories of his early days while he was working with his father. He would go out all night, come home, change into his work clothes, and then he would welcome a crack across the back of his head from his father as they got into the truck to go to work. He received the crack for staying out at night, never for being late.

Rudy and I both benefitted from the guidance of our fathers keeping us straight.

When Rudy was a young man, employment was a little tougher to come by. Rudy shared that it was even tougher for an Italian. Rudy spoke of factories in Chicago that had help wanted signs with the disclaimer that Italians need not apply. Rudy's father was a bricklayer, and although bricklaying is a difficult trade, it is an honest trade. Italians were welcome in this trade.

Rudy had a few other career paths between bricklaying and becoming a carpenter. Those middle endeavors worked well for a while. The problem with those other careers was that they didn't provide a sustainable living, especially for a guy with a young family.

Rudy would tell me stories of his days working at one of his jobs. As a young man, I was quite captivated listening to Rudy's stories. Although the stories were captivating, they didn't provide any tangible career lessons, except, maybe, to get a real job.

Rudy had quite a few sayings, and he always repeated them throughout the day. There were two sayings that were my favorites, and they have stayed with me.

The first one Rudy would say was "chicken today, feathers tomorrow." He would say this when we knew there would be an impending crew size reduction at the end of an event. Some guys would be cut, and I suppose just like a chicken after it had been butchered, there wouldn't be much left of them but the feathers.

I am a little embarrassed to say that it took a few times of hearing it before I knew what Rudy meant when he would say this. Today, the message might be said a little differently, probably more commonly phrased as "you're only as good as your last project."

My second favorite Rudy sayings was "you have two ears and one mouth; there's a reason for that." This was his way of telling the young guys to be quiet, work, and listen to him and the other experienced senior members of the crew who knew more than we did. I believe Rudy must have done a lot of listening when he was a young man, and he made up for it, as he did a lot of talking as one of the senior members of our crew.

Rudy always looked out for everyone's safety too.

We often used flat trucks to tote our supplies around on the show floor. A typical flat truck has a thirty-two-inch-by-sixty-inch deck with caster wheels with the deck about eight inches from the floor. The handle to push and steer the flat truck was about thirty-two inches high on one side of the deck of the flat truck, with the caster wheels that allow the cart to be steered under the handle.

Rudy always made sure that the crew was pushing the flat truck with the deck in front, not pulling it with the deck behind the person who was pulling it. Rudy didn't want to see anyone have their heels caught up on the flat truck as they pulled it. I saw it happen once to someone, and it took him quite a while to walk off the pain.

I look back and realize that every day working with Rudy was a good day. He was a great coach and a good man. I miss those days, and I would welcome another day of working with him and listening to his stories.

The Career Lesson: When you're new, pay attention to the veterans; they know what they are doing.

The second Career Lesson: Listening to the senior members on the team is worthwhile, and then, someday you will realize how much you miss them and be thankful to have spent time with them when you did.

20
Jimmy the Greek

Jimmy the Greek was my father's friend and is still my friend.

Jimmy the Greek was, as one would surmise, from Greece. Jimmy had a love for the sea that began as a child, as he and his father were fisherman in the Mediterranean Sea. He then joined the merchant marine as a carpenter, building decking structures in the grain holds of the ocean ships. As Jimmy the Greek shared with me, the decks were built to keep the grain from shifting in the high seas. The decks Jimmy built kept the grain level so the ship sailed level. Upon reaching the port for the delivery of the grain, Jimmy would dismantle the decks.

While in the merchant marine, Jimmy sailed all around the world, which brought him to the United States. I am not sure—and I have never asked him—how a sailor who loved the sea ended up landlocked in the middle of the continent. As Chicago became his home, like many people in Chicago, Jimmy spent a lot of his free time on his boat fishing in Lake Michigan.

In the late seventies, trade shows were feast and famine, which meant my father and Jimmy did a lot of side jobs together to keep money rolling in when there weren't any shows to work. They would hear of an opportunity, and next thing I knew, I would be helping them on a side job, cutting trees down, roofing a house, painting a hair salon, or remodeling a kitchen. I was a young teenager then and always tagged along and did the busy work and earned a few bucks along the way.

Jimmy and my father were resourceful. They did not know how to cut down trees when they got their first tree job, but they bought chainsaws and learned as they went along. Cutting trees is a technical and dangerous task, but they always got the job done, and their clients were always pleased. They always presented themselves as knowledgeable professionals and were convincing during the sale.

When Jimmy and my Father had a large tree to cut, it was up to Jimmy to climb the tree and trim the high branches. Jimmy was thin and in great shape, with the natural ability to carry a chainsaw while climbing to the highest points in a tree. None of this was an easy task, but Jimmy was a determined individual, and he got the job done.

When I was older and joined my father as a carpenter working trade shows, I spent a lot of time working with and for Jimmy the Greek. Jimmy was a natural mentor, and he led by example. He was a dedicated worker who always did the job right and to his high standards. All one had to do was to keep up and do what Jimmy did to be doing the right thing themselves.

Jimmy was a great leader on the job. Usually, when we think of great leaders, we think of the person giving the orders and monitoring the production. Jimmy was a hands-on leader. When you worked on Jimmy's crew, he set an efficient working tempo with an emphasis on doing the task to his high standards. Working with a leader like Jimmy meant you upped your game, as you didn't want to disappoint him.

There were quite a few guys who started on Jimmy's crew but didn't last. You kept up with Jimmy or you would find yourself weeded out and on another crew. The general foreman knew if you could keep up with Jimmy, you were someone he could rely on when there were tasks that needed to be done fast and correctly. Jimmy's good reputation extended to his crew.

Jimmy never did anything halfway either; he always completed tasks the right way, which also happened to be his way. Whatever Jimmy was building, he built it to last. I know, because he was not shy about telling me or anyone else how to do something or how to redo it so it would be up to his standards.

In his version of English, Jimmy would state the way he expected you to do things, which were always to do it the right way, which also happened to be Jimmy's way. If you thought four nails were enough to hold two panels together, Jimmy would tell you to sink six nails in the panels.

Even though Jimmy may not have always used the right words and was sometimes hard to understand, everyone knew what he was saying. Jimmy wanted it done right, as he took great pride in the work he and his crew did.

Jimmy always gave an honest day's work and he earned an honest day's pay. When you were on Jimmy's crew, you did the same too. When someone on the crew slacked off, that someone, along with the English language, took a verbal beating.

The Career Lesson: Take pride in the work you and your crew are doing. Following a leader like Jimmy The Greek may not be easy; however, the education you will gain and the extension of their reputation to yours is well worth it.

Thank you, Jimmy the Greek.

21
Big Jim

Big Jim was a senior executive who I was fortunate to work and travel with on many different events for quite a few years. Working with Big Jim allowed me to see almost every major city in the United States and a few cities in Canada too. Big Jim was a great mentor and an even better friend.

I had many great experiences with Big Jim, and I learned a lot while working with him, so we are going to be with the Big Jim for a while.

Well known in the trade show industry as an accomplished diplomat, Big Jim was able to negotiate many good agreements. When negotiations were difficult, Big Jim may not have won outright, but he was always able to negotiate, at the minimum, an agreement that was workable for us and not much better for our partners. Big Jim was sharp.

My partnership with Big Jim was the result of my father having worked with him. As Big Jim liked my father, I had an inside advantage with Big Jim when I started. While working with and for my father, I had the opportunity for exposure with Big Jim on a few events.

Our partnership really started on one particular event that allowed me to emerge from my father's shadow and stand on my own with Big Jim. This opportunity was another two-story exhibit installation in McCormick Place. It was a first-time build for this particular exhibit, and the installation on show site was proving to be a difficult job.

The exhibit featured a second level that was accessible by two sets of spiral stairs. The second level featured offices, and the wall components of the offices had been fabricated in a shop separate from the steel deck. The office walls were delivered to show site without ever having been assembled on the steel deck—that is, until they were assembled together during install on show site.

To nobody's surprise, the second level wall components were not fitting on the deck as designed on the plans. As we were adjusting things to fit on site, the installation required long days to complete, which meant a lot of overtime. Overtime always concerned Big Jim, as it was cutting into the profit.

After several long days of installation, we were getting close to finishing with the show opening the next day. With being close to finishing the build-out, my assignment that evening was to install double swing bar doors for the offices on the second level of the exhibit structure. The doors were half-inch-thick, smoked acrylic panels, and they were quite heavy. Each door had two double swing door hinges that I needed to affix to the doorframes with screws.

Double swing door hinges are hinges that allow a door to swing both inside and outside the office. The best description of the doors is that they were similar to the doors one would have seen in an old western movie at the entrance to a saloon, except that they were smoked acrylic, not made of wood louvers like in the movies. The doors were about forty-two inches tall, and when installed, the bottom of the doors was to be thirty-six inches from the floor. Once installed, there was enough solid door panel at eye level so that a person walking by the office could not see clearly into the room.

While working, we were typically paired up with a partner on these types of tasks; however, the partner I was paired up to work with was not working with me. My supposed partner may have been upset that my father was the lead foreman on the job, as he believed it should have been him. Because of his perceived slight and my being the foreman's son, my so-called partner wouldn't work with me; thus I was working alone.

The task of installing a door that swings both ways is fairly simple with four hands. The task became rather difficult as I was by myself with only two hands.

Here is a brief description of the task.

We had already installed the hinges onto the doors prior to mounting the doors to the doorjambs. Installing the doors to the doorjambs required quite a few actions. The first action was to hold the door from the bottom at the correct height while keeping it plumb (straight up and down) by resting it against your forehead; the next step was to drill pilot holes through the hinge to then be able insert the screws through the hinges and then screw them into the doorjamb.

This was difficult for me to explain in words, and I hope I explained it well enough for you to understand the scope of the task. As difficult as this was for me to describe, you can imagine how difficult it was to do in practice.

Admittedly, I am not the best carpenter to have walked the trade show floor, so it wasn't going well for me. The installation occurred before we had battery powered drills, which meant I was using a drill with a cord. While I was installing the doors, I placed the drill at arm's height on a nearby ladder step so I could easily grab it when needed. The height at which I placed the drill on the ladder was reachable from my position while holding the door in place; however, the cord of the drill descended to the floor and kept getting in my way.

Just as I was ready to grab the drill to bore the pilot holes, I hit the cord of the drill with my foot, and the drill fell off the ladder. The drill fell, breaking the drill bit off upon hitting the floor. Luckily we had one more drill bit the right size, so I went to the tool box and was able to replace the broken drill bit with a new one to keep working.

With the new drill bit placed in the drill, I was back to the balancing act of holding the door. The door was in my left hand in the correct upright position, balanced plumb, resting with my forehead on the door while reaching for the drill positioned on the nearby ladder with my right hand. Once again, I hit the cord and the drill fell, but this time it landed on the top of my foot. I picked up the drill and discovered the last drill bit was broken off. I hadn't even drilled one hole yet to hang a door.

As the drill bits were about two inches long, I reasoned I could find one of the broken-off parts of the drill bit on the floor of the office I was working in. Once found, the broken drill bit would be inserted it into the drill, and it would have been long enough to bore the pilot holes and finish installing the doors.

With a backup plan in place, I started to walk around the office, looking on the floor for either of the two broken drill bits. The area I was looking in wasn't too big, about six feet by eight feet; however, the more I walked around looking for one of the two drill bits, the more my foot began to hurt.

I was finally able to locate one of the drill bits and simultaneously discovered the reason my foot was hurting. When the drill fell the second time, hitting my foot, the drill bit actually impaled me between the shoelace eyes of my work boot. This is where the drill bit broke off after landing on my foot. I discovered this as there was about an eighth of an inch of the drill bit sticking out of my boot.

At this point my supposed partner became helpful, and while sporting a wide grin, offered to pull the drill bit out of my foot with his pliers. I declined the offer and accepted another offer to go to the hospital to have a trained healthcare professional take care of it. It was about 8:00 p.m., and it was off to the emergency room.

In the hospital, the doctor wanted to cut my work boot off my foot, however, I was able to convince him to see if he could pull the drill bit and save my boot. The doctor had my foot x-rayed and discovered that the drill bit had missed the bones, so he then pulled the drill bit out of my foot with his pliers.

I appreciated the doctor taking care of this, as he didn't grin while he extracted the drill bit from my foot. As an added bonus, my work boots were still in good shape.

The one bright spot during the hospital visit occurred when several nurses came into my room to make sure I was okay.

Lucky for me, it wasn't a bad wound, and there wasn't much that could be done other than to disinfect it and apply a simple Band-Aid to the spot where the drill bit had impaled me. That was it. I walked out of the hospital a little sore, but walking in my work boots.

The next morning was show opening, and I felt good enough to join the crew at 4:00 a.m. installing aisle carpet. Admittedly, I was interested in the premium pay and didn't want to miss out on it. I was also young enough that working through any discomfort I may have had was still easy.

This whole experience wasn't as bad as it sounded; however, when Big Jim heard about it the next morning, he was impressed. In his experience, when situations like this had happened to other men and they had been hurt, it usually resulted in a workman's comp claim and weeks off work with pay to recover. In other words, some people may have turned it into a paid vacation.

Big Jim stated that he wanted me on his crew after he heard I had returned to install aisle carpet after having my foot impaled by a drill bit. I suppose when you hear a person has been impaled, it sounds a lot worse than it actually is.

The Career Lesson: Dedication to the job and doing the right thing will be noticed, and sometimes is noticed by the right people. Sometimes that someone will make a big difference in your career. Although it's been said many times, I'll say it again: do the right thing, even when you don't think anyone is watching.

I traveled to Miami Beach for quite a few shows with Big Jim. I always enjoyed Miami Beach, especially when "Miami Vice" was on TV. For the most part, inside the convention center, it was another typical convention center building; outside of the convention center, Miami Beach was a happening place to be.

Working in the Miami Beach Convention Center was a unique experience back in the day. The crew was very diverse: there were New Yorkers, Cubans, and people from South America mixed in with the local Floridians. Being from out of town and from Chicago meant it took a little time to get to know the crew and trust each other. Once the ice was broken, they were good guys and we all got along fine. It also took a little time to gain their respect to do things per the plan.

Before departing for one particular trip to Miami, Big Jim had informed me and my partner Ron Jon, who was also from Chicago, that he had cut a deal with the local union to allow us to work with our tools. We would be able to do more than just supervise. We were happy about this, as while on the road, it was sometimes easier to do the work ourselves than try to explain it to someone who was new to the job.

In some cases, the local crews knew how to do the work just fine; they just chose to do it a little slower. In the trade show industry, and I am sure in other industries, when there are more hours worked, there is more money made by extending the time it takes to complete the job than by just completing it efficiently.

Upon the first day of move-in, and with the green light from Big Jim having coordinated with the local union, we started working with our tools. Within five minutes of starting that morning, the local union steward made a beeline to us and asked what in the "bebop" did we think we were doing in his city! His words were a little stronger, but we'll keep everything PG here. We responded that Big Jim had made a deal to allow us to work and we were just doing as Big Jim had worked out with his union.

Our explanation only seemed to upset him even more, and after he had laid into us some more, we went back to put our tools away and inform Big Jim that the steward wasn't aware of his deal. We invited Big Jim to speak to the steward and explain the deal he had made for us to work. Big Jim didn't take us up on the offer to meet the steward; he just shrugged his shoulders, opened his hands, and smiled his smile with the sparkle in his eyes.

We went back to supervising, knowing Big Jim probably hadn't made any deal. We were young and gullible, and Big Jim had us testing the waters to see if we could get away with working in another union's jurisdiction. It took a little time, and the union steward came around and became friendly with us. He was satisfied with his informative dissertation on the local rules, and his crew saw him laying us out, so they were satisfied too. He also saw that we were abiding by the local rules.

The Career Lesson: We were put out there to test the limits of the local rules, and we didn't pass the test. As time went by, I learned to read the tea leaves better.

During the move-in on another event in New Orleans, Big Jim had assigned me to build portable, soundproof meeting rooms on the show floor. The rooms were purpose built to provide a place to demonstrate musical instruments on the show floor in a somewhat soundproof environment. The construction of the rooms included collecting the components for each of the rooms from a stack of materials in the boneyard at show site and supervising a local crew in New Orleans to assemble them.

Back when this event occurred, we didn't have CAD drawings or detailed pull lists, so knowledge of the materials was key. These rooms were new to me, as I hadn't ever actually built one of these portable meeting rooms. I was learning every day, and this day was no different.

Upon starting this task, I discovered that the corner posts and wall panels weren't matching the length of the ceiling beams and ceiling panels, thus impacting our ability to construct the room. The beams were too short to span the walls, as the walls and corner posts that were sent to us weren't the correct mix of parts. As we weren't able to complete the rooms efficiently with the parts on hand, we had to make onsite adjustments which required additional time to complete the rooms.

At this point, I had to update Big Jim on the situation and the additional time it was taking to complete the rooms. This was not a conversation I was looking forward to, as I was not delivering good news. The team back in Chicago that had pulled the materials had pulled mismatched components.

As to be expected, Big Jim was not happy to hear the news I delivered. The explanation for the delay didn't matter to Big Jim either; all he heard was that this was going to delay completion and delivery to the clients and add cost to the project.

Big Jim's response consisted of his venting at me. The longer Big Jim vented, the madder he became, and the madder he became, the tighter his lips were and the quieter he spoke. As he continued with his venting and speaking ever more softly, I needed to lean in closer and closer to him so I could hear my chewing out. Fun times, to say the least.

Back to the job at hand. We were able to source the needed components locally and then completed the rooms without too much delay or added cost. By the time the task was completed, Big Jim had cooled down and learned that the mistake was upstream from my position and that I wasn't at fault for the difficulties.

Big Jim never apologized for the chewing-out he doled to me. Instead, he gave me that great smile with the sparkle in his eyes as he welcomed me back to the jobsite office at the end of the day. Everything was good.

The Career Lesson: if there is a mistake, work toward the solution; don't get bogged down on whose fault it was and whether you received a proper apology. Look ahead and leave the mistake behind.

On one of our many trips to Louisville, I discovered one of the greatest gifts Big Jim had. I have practiced it myself many times; however, I am certain I am not as good as he was at it.

In Louisville, we worked at a facility that included the fairgrounds and a basketball arena for the Cardinals, and it was also a convention center. The event we worked occurred in November and occupied every bit of exhibit space they could use. Without any spare space on the show floor, we were lucky to be able to place our onsite offices in the locker rooms in the arena. The locker rooms were not a pleasant-smelling space, but it was out of the cold and quiet.

Being in a convention center with limited services for eighteen days, we would set up a coffee maker in our locker room office. The coffee maker was more than the typical Mr. Coffee pot; it had three burners so you could have more than one pot of coffee going at a time. As with any work-related coffee area, it became a meeting place, and most everyone was welcome. This included our staff, the clients, and the staff from the facility.

As the convention center was a state-managed facility, we coordinated with various state employees to produce the event. The facility staff performed many different tasks depending on what type of event was in the facility. When we arrived and began setting up our trade show, the facility staff were still cleaning the remnants of the previous livestock event.

The task of cleaning up after a livestock show included removing the portable corrals, washing the walls, and a lot of floor cleaning. Then for our event, the staff proceeded to deliver exhibit freight for the exhibitors. They were also the groundskeepers and did everything else that was required to maintain the facility.

The leader of the facility crew was a guy named Red. Red and I were on a tip-the-head and nod-to-each-other-as-we-pass basis. Red was not a big conversationalist, and we didn't have too many verbal interactions to develop a relationship. Suffice it to say, Red was a nice guy and a good leader who was well liked and respected by his crew.

Red's son was part of his crew, and as best I could tell, he was one of the higher ranking members, as he was always able to stay on his forklift. I never noticed Red's son on any of the crews doing the manual cleanup. I didn't know what Red's sons name was, but he was a hard-working guy who was always wearing a Carhartt one-piece, insulated work suit, and he had a long beard and long hair.

Where this all comes together is that Red was one of the many welcome visitors to the coffee pot. Red's son was a new visitor and wasn't quite comfortable with going in the office yet. With the coffee made and ready to pour, everyone, including Red's son, received a warm welcome from Big Jim when they came in to fill up.

Big Jim's eyes lit up, and with a big smile he welcomed Red and his son into the office and offered them a cup of coffee. I noticed this, as it was the same big smile and warm welcome I had just received when I walked into the office. Big Jim had the gift of making everybody he had contact with feel special and welcome.

It was then that I remembered one of the first things Big Jim had told me. Early in his career, Big Jim learned to be good to everyone, starting with the doorman as you walked into a building. Then keep up the kindness with everyone you met along the way, as you didn't know when you might need to rely on one of these folks for a favor. He lived this philosophy.

> **The Career Lesson:** A warm smile, happy eyes, and a generous welcome can make anyone feel good. Being nice doesn't cost a thing; a cup of coffee is pretty cheap, and both can open a lot of doors.

I have to give Big Jim a lot of the credit for my successful transition from carpenter to account executive. While I was still a carpenter, Big Jim began using me as an account executive at show site. His favorite account executive had moved to New York, and he needed someone to be his eyes and ears on the floor.

The best part for Big Jim was that once the day was ending, I was still able to put my tools on and jump on the aisle carpet crew in the evening.

With Big Jim, I had access to the clients and managed the onsite elements of the events when we worked together. Big Jim was still in charge, but this arrangement gave me a head start in my next endeavor.

> **The Career Lesson:** While I was still a carpenter, Big Jim had me doing the job I have now. The experience I gained with Big Jim helped me successfully transition to my new position when it became official. Take the challenge when it is offered to you regardless of the pay or title; greater opportunities may present once you have proven yourself.

The one box Big Jim was not able to check with me while on his crew was that I didn't marry an exhibitor services representative from the company. Big Jim was crafty when it came to costs, especially hotel costs, and any time he could get a two-for-one in a room, I think he felt he was ahead.

In fact, as Big Jim was so crafty with the hotel costs, we had to stay at a few very unique places.

On a trip to Houston, we had to use our screw guns to screw our windows shut, as the windows wouldn't lock, and the district we were in was one where you wanted your windows to be locked. Big Jim's go-to comment to justify the poor state of the room was that it didn't really matter anyway; all we needed to do there was sleep in the room. He would also add that we weren't on vacation.

In Louisville, Big Jim would put us in a hotel that faced Interstate 65. The building and parking lot of the hotel was fenced in by a six-foot-tall chain-link fence with a run of spooled barbwire at the top. The doors of the hotel rooms opened to the parking lot for easy access too. Inside, the rooms had the multicolor shag carpet, and you never needed to worry about falling out of bed, as the mattresses were quite sunken in where one would sleep. The only good thing about this hotel was that we were across the street from a twenty-four-hour donut shop with good coffee. The finest of accommodations, to say the least.

Luckily, in Louisville, we eventually upgraded from the spooled barbwire-fenced parking lot hotel to a newly built hotel closer to the fairgrounds where we were working. Although this hotel was newer, it still had doors that opened to the parking lot.

As the hotel was convenient to the fairgrounds, my partner Ron Jon and I ran to each of our rooms one day during lunch, where I found the maid in my room with her boyfriend. That's kind of weird, but it gets weirder.

When I entered the room, I found that the maid's boyfriend had my pants on him. I politely asked the boyfriend to leave, and to leave my pants. The maid and the boyfriend apologized and claimed they were just trying to determine what size pants the boyfriend fit in, as he needed to buy new pants. To the boyfriend's credit, he was nice about the situation and left my pants. If you were wondering, my pants the boyfriend had on fit him fairly well.

A couple days later, Ron Jon was looking for the new pair of pants that he had brought to wear for the show opening. After looking through his suitcase, Ron Jon realized that his pants were gone. The maid's boyfriend had found his new pants in his size in Ron Jon's room!

The Career Lesson: I am not sure if there are any lessons here. I used to get upset about the junky hotels, but now I am able to look back and laugh about it.

In Louisville, one of the local crew members Big Jim had recruited who was especially important to us also happened to work a full-time gig with a theatrical lighting company. Although this crew member had a full-time gig, he stayed on this show out of respect for Big Jim. With this crew member in the lighting business, it worked out well, as we always had a place to source lights when an exhibitor wanted to rent lights to highlight an RV.

In addition to the theatrical lighting, this crew member was very productive and a great asset to our team. One of the benefits for this crew member and his wife was that they were able to work with each other on this event. The crew member's wife didn't work full time, but with this being a November show that we were working, she found that the additional cash before the holidays was pretty handy.

When Big Jim began handing more of the reins for overseeing this event over to me, this crew member decided it was his time to exit the crew. His regular theatrical light job had become steady work, and he really only came down to work this event because he liked Big Jim and his wife liked the work.

When this crew member mentioned to me that he would be stepping down, I didn't want to lose him, as we relied on him for the resources he had access to. I asked him to reconsider and stay for a couple more years; however, his mind was made up.

As I knew how much his wife enjoyed working the gig, I asked Big Jim if we could provide the wife a raise. Big Jim smiled and agreed with this strategy, as he knew this might work in keeping this crew member on the team.

After Big Jim and I had agreed on the plan, I visited with the wife and shared that we were very pleased with everything she was doing, and I stated we felt she was deserving of a pay increase.

She was one of the nicest people I have known, and receiving the recognition was a big deal for her. The raise was important, but the recognition was what really made her happy. Looking back, I see she was a hard worker and deserved the bump in pay anyway.

A couple hours later, the crew member caught up with me and told me his wife had shared the good news. He also shared that between the two of us, it was only check, not checkmate. He would be around a few more years, as he didn't want to disappoint his wife, as she was so proud and happy with the recognition and raise she had earned. He kept his word; a couple years later he did make his exit; however, he stayed on long enough to allow us to find an alternative solution for the theatrical lighting.

I still think about the smile the wife had when we thanked her for the great job she was doing when we provided the pay increase.

The Career Lesson: This was an example of the lessons I learned from working with Big Jim over the years. Never stop looking for a way to make people feel good while achieving your objective.

There is a story that includes negotiations that Big Jim had that enabled the Chicago team to work in Louisville. The crew in Louisville were skilled and competent; however, if there was a theater show or movie filming in town, the most skilled seniority crew would take that call. Big Jim had lived through this in many cities, and as he was smart, he always liked to take some of his home-field-advantage team on the road to cover his bases.

Many years earlier, Big Jim had discovered one of the members of the local crew in a difficult situation, and Big Jim had made a deal with him to allow the Chicago crew to work alongside the Louisville crew. Once the agreement had been finalized, the difficult situation had been dropped, and everyone had become one happy crew.

Big Jim had looked beyond the present difficulties of this situation, used it to his advantage, and made a deal for a better and long-term resolution. Big Jim played the long game.

The resolution Big Jim had applied that enabled the Chicago team to work with the Louisville crew could have been used as an example in an international diplomacy class at the best university. We were outsiders, and by leveraging an equitable agreement, Jim broke down the barriers for us to become one team!

The Career Lesson: Leveraging a difficult situation to an equitable agreement, without hurting the other side, is how Big Jim created win-win situations.

22
Old Hickory

I am not sure how Old Hickory gained his nickname, but I think it may be for one or both of the following reasons. The first reason was obvious, as he had a head full of gray hair. The second reason may have been that under his gray hair, his head was as hard as a hickory tree trunk. The more I think about it, the more I think it may have been because he was hard headed.

Old Hickory didn't talk a lot, and he didn't need to say much to get his point across. Old Hickory was very efficient with his words; he pretty much said exactly what he was thinking. Old Hickory was also efficient with his actions. He didn't move fast, but he accomplished a lot while working. Every task Old Hickory started was completed in a timely manner, and the task was always done exactly to specification.

It was always good to be on Old Hickory's crew. Old Hickory always did the right thing, as he had a great moral compass that guided him. Old Hickory knew what was right and what was wrong. He always did what was right and didn't deal with the gray areas while at work.

This was an impressive quality to have, as where we worked it was a gray world, and it would have been easy to just accept things that went against his values. Old Hickory was a good man to work with, and his strong will and moral strength kept me, and quite a few others, doing the right thing at the right time.

There aren't many men who stand strong every day for what is right. Old Hickory always stood strong, and I feel fortunate to have stood with him.

The Career Lesson: Some people have a natural inner strength and always stand for what is right. It's always good to stand with people who have this strength.

23
The Louisville Crew

I worked with a skilled and a hard-working crew while producing shows in Louisville, Kentucky. I worked with this crew on an annual basis on a particular event for about twelve years. While working in Louisville, and thanks to these men, I learned a valuable lesson.

Before going to Louisville to work my first show, I was thinking I was a sophisticated, cool guy from the big city of Chicago. I did not go to Louisville with great expectations of working with the country bumpkins of Kentucky. Once there, I found that many of these men were in fact from the country and also worked their own farms or businesses.

When there was work in the exhibit hall or local theaters, they came into the city and worked the events. The show we worked together was in late November and helped everyone on the Louisville crew earn a few extra paychecks just in time for the holidays

The first thing I learned from the crew in Louisville is that they were dedicated to doing a good job. In many cases, they were willing to bring materials and special tools from their home to complete a task when they thought their resources would help. They were also pretty good at making sure their contributions were reciprocated, and there was a fair amount of negotiating going on.

As an example, if we needed lumber to complete an activation, they were happy to bring it to the job, and in return, after the show, they would leave with a little carpet for someone's house. Overall, it was an equitable transaction, as we were able to complete our task on time, and then we saved on return shipping, with less carpet going back to Chicago.

The second and most important lesson I learned from these men is how smart they were. They spoke slowly and never talked about their education or their lack of education. Although they didn't talk about their education, I knew they valued an education, as many of their children were either college graduates, in college, or college bound. They were proud to share and talk about their children's achievements in education.

Many of these men weren't book-smart, but they were smart in building things and fixing things, and they were expert negotiators and intelligent human beings.

Not only were the men from Louisville smart; they were strategic too.

As I mentioned earlier, I thought I was sophisticated, being from Chicago, and I really looked up to some of the older members on the Chicago crew. I thought they were the apex of sophistication. The Chicago crew talked big and did a lot of bragging, and I bought into their BS at the beginning of my career.

Some of the Chicago crew I looked up to were big gamblers, as they spent a lot of time going to Las Vegas and the local horse tracks. They were always bragging about how great they did and all the money they were winning. They were very animated when they talked about their gambling success, and I was drawn in and in awe of them.

The Louisville crew didn't go to Las Vegas, but they liked to gamble. They had a standing poker game every weekend to satisfy their gambling needs. The Louisville crew may have been country; however, they played the Chicago crew for the overconfident and "easy pickins" they were.

The Chicago crew I looked up to bought into the Louisville crew's good-ole-country boy trap and thought they were going to clean out those hapless country boys. I heard there were some big poker games going on with these groups.

At the end of the trip, a couple of the Chicago crew left owing big markers that they couldn't settle in one paycheck. In fact, one guy couldn't set foot in town without looking over his shoulder, as he didn't make good on his markers. Every year after, when I returned to Louisville, I would learn who owned the markers, as the markers were sold down within the Louisville crew until the markers weren't worth anything.

The Louisville crew demonstrated that there are book smarts and also experience smarts. From them I learned that an education isn't a measure for intelligence. They knew how to read people, and they played the long game. The Louisville crew played the country bumpkin act all the way to the bank with their newly won Chicago money. They never did any bragging about it either, as they didn't want to spoil their ruse with the next smart guy from Chicago.

As a side note, I found it a little strange that the men from Louisville didn't consider themselves southerners. Coming from Chicago, I considered Louisville to be the South, as they sure talked different there. As I traveled further into the South, I realized that there are several definitions of being from the South, and each definition is relative to how far north you are coming from.

The Career Lesson: Intelligence isn't predicated by an education or how fast one talks. When someone is talking slowly, it is a good indication that they are thinking fast. Intelligence is equally distributed.

24
It Ain't Easy

I sometimes wonder how someone who has no prior knowledge of the trade show industry assimilates into it. We had one account person who was very smart and was good at the paperwork end of the gig but really did not understand the mechanics of show site.

There were a few folks who joked about it, but I didn't think it was fair. There are still times I encounter situations where I need to step back and think about the tactics of doing something. When this happens, I always wonder how someone new to the industry handles these situations.

There was a situation like that for this account person, and I was activated to help out. We were able to find a solution to whatever it was, and we had the problem solved. I don't recall what the challenge was; however, I do remember that the account executive graciously thanked me when it was done.

It was a heartfelt thank-you, too. There weren't a lot of thank-yous back then, and I still recall it like it happened yesterday.

The Career Lesson: I don't recall anything about what I did that day; however, I will always remember the thank-you for it. Gratitude makes a difference.

25
Big Ron

Big Ron was the general foreman I worked for on a consistent basis. As the general foreman, Big Ron didn't need to put his tools on and do physical work very often; however, he had one of the hardest jobs in the business. If there was a show we were working in Chicago, Big Ron was first on and last off. He spent a lot of time in the exhibit hall.

Big Ron wasn't a big guy. My father told me Big Ron gained the "big" in his name as there were two Rons before I started, and the other Ron was Little Ron. Little Ron was the smaller Ron of the two Rons, so "big" and "little" became the default differentiator between the two Rons. Most people didn't know him as Big Ron, as Little Ron had moved on a few years earlier. The only reason I knew of it was from hearing from my father when I was a child as he talked about work.

Not only was Big Ron there almost every day; he had to hire everyone when there was work and let everyone go when the work ran out. For most people, being hired and fired wasn't as bad as it sounds. Once there was work again, we were all rehired.

There were some guys that didn't understand why they were consistently hired last and let go first.

Those hired-last and fired-first guys knew there were other guys working more than they were. It never occurred to them that they might move up in rankings if they put in a little extra effort and were consistent in their attendance and punctuality. I don't think they were self-aware enough to realize they had the power to move up in the crew by putting more effort in. Either way, it must have been hard for Big Ron to maintain balance with the crew.

When one of the members of the crew wasn't pulling their weight or giving an honest day's work, something would have to be done. In a typical job, there might be a one-on-one discussion with the boss with a note in the file, but this wasn't the typical job. Soon the member of the crew who wasn't giving an honest day's work would find they were hired later in the move-in and were let go earlier in the move-out, thus working fewer hours.

Many of the men figured it out and straightened out, and then they were back to being in their normal place on the crew. Some men didn't figure it out on their own, and sooner or later, they found they were working a lot less or they weren't working at all. Their place on the crew was filled by someone who was able to make it on time and gave an honest day's work.

If someone was slacking, Big Ron never had to fire them; he just rehired them less and less until they figured it out and straightened up or went somewhere else.

Big Ron also had a lot of pressure to hire everyone's relative, and—full disclosure—I was my father's son, thus a relative too. Luckily for me, in the eighties, the trade show business was growing fast, and hardworking people were always in demand.

This being a part-time job with a good wage, there was also a subset of the crew who wanted to work just enough to support the activities they indulged in while they were on their own time. Many of these men did not want to keep a steady job; they just needed enough to finance their next endeavor.

Once they had enough money in their pocket, they checked out, which was usually when the show opened. Then, when the show closed, they checked back in for tear-down just as they were running out of money and needed more money to finance their next endeavor. As long as these men gave an honest day's work, were on time, and didn't miss a call, they were always needed, hired, and appreciated.

Big Ron had a big job managing a big cast of characters.

Finally, Big Ron gave me a piece of advice that I wish I had followed when he gave it to me. While I was still a young man, Big Ron advised me to open an IRA. He told me it would be a great thing for me, and he wished he had had the opportunity to do this when he was a young man.

At the time, I didn't know what an IRA was and didn't act on it. Quite honestly, I didn't even know where to go to open an account. Back when Big Ron gave me the advice, I had just bought my first house, and I was worried about making the mortgage payments. Frankly, I didn't expect to grow older and need to think about retirement either.

Although I didn't follow Big Ron's advice for myself, I never forget it, as his advice echoes louder in my head every year that passes.

Believe me, I am still mad at myself for not listening to him. There are second chances, and I have applied his good advice and convinced my daughter Madisyn to open her own Roth IRA at twenty-one. I did not benefit from his good advice, but my daughter will. It was good advice then and is still good advice now.

The Career Lesson: Trade show labor is in good company: actors, athletes, and coaches are all hired to be fired, and then to be rehired when the work returns. Big Ron proved to be a fair and good foreman, and just like a good coach, he built a great team.

The Life Lesson: Listen to good advice; when you are young, save for the future, as it is the best time to save, considering the compounding interest.

26
The Cowboy

By silhouette the Cowboy was the spitting image of John Wayne in every cowboy movie the Duke ever made. The Cowboy was about six foot four, wore cowboy boots, jeans, shirts with the pearl snaps instead of buttons, and of course, a cowboy hat. His face was as worn as the boots he had on, and he had a permanent squint to his eyes. The Cowboy usually had a Marlboro burning away between his lips.

I had the misfortune of having a task that seriously affected the Cowboy's ability to do his job.

The Cowboy was in charge of delivering freight into meeting rooms on both floors of the center meeting rooms at the Las Vegas Convention Center. Delivering the freight is the first task during move-in; the second freight task includes the removal of the empty crates once the exhibits have been set. Upon the close of the show, the freight team will return the empty crates, and then once they are repacked and ready, the freight team will move out the full crates and load them onto trucks.

Moving freight into and out of meeting rooms is never easy, and the difficulty of the task was compounded by having to use an elevator to access the second floor, and there aren't any real docks in this location. This occurred during a major event, and if you are familiar with the Las Vegas Convention Center, you know the center meeting rooms are located at the far and lowest end of the center hall lobby. The meeting room hallways have two entrances from the center lobby, as the meeting room hallway is a U shape, with both ends originating in the center lobby.

For my task, I would arrive in Las Vegas the day after Christmas and then began supervising the building of the sound rooms rented to exhibitors the next day. The sound rooms were available to exhibitors so they would be able to demonstrate stereos and sound systems in them without disturbing everyone around them. We would start building the sound rooms in the center lobby first. As the sound rooms in the center lobby were completed, the last four sound rooms we had to build were in the bottom U section of the first floor meeting room hallway.

The last three sound rooms were close to the roll-up freight door, and the fourth sound room blocked the roll-up freight door. The fourth room happened to block the freight door the Cowboy was working from to move his freight.

Those last four sound rooms had to be built and completed to provide enough time for the occupant of the sound room to set up their gear in it to be show ready for show opening the next morning. To allow the exhibitors enough time to set up, I would be blocking the Cowboy's door in the late afternoon the day before show opening, a hectic time for everyone, especially the Cowboy.

When I would turn the corner with the crew to build those last four rooms, and particularly the one that blocked the roll-up freight door, the Cowboy would give me a piercing stare-down and sneer before turning away while muttering something under his breath to his crew. His crew would all look up at me, so whatever the Cowboy said didn't make anyone happy or glad to see me turning the corner.

I don't think the Cowboy realized I wasn't responsible for assigning the booths on the floor plan that were blocking the door he needed at a critical part of his finishing the freight operation. It didn't matter to him; I was the person in front of him, and he sure blamed me for disrupting his operation.

The Cowboy and I kept this uneasy arrangement up for about seven years. He would see me and knew I was the reason his freight door was closing before he was finished. We didn't speak much, as we had an understanding that required both of us to do a job we weren't happy about. The Cowboy didn't want me closing his door, and I didn't want to be closing his door and catching his grief.

Once I arrived and started building the last room the Cowboy was working from a double pedestrian door that didn't allow forklifts to efficiently pass in and out, thus making his crew's job much more physically difficult. I would finish the sound rooms, and the Cowboy and crew were still pulling empties late into the night.

One thing the Cowboy always had was a coffee pot tucked away in a nook near his desk. As the days were long and I enjoyed playing a little blackjack in the evenings, I was pretty tired by the end of a long move-in. The LVCC, like most convention centers, is a bit of an island for services. Suffice it to say I sure could have used a cup of coffee. As I was the guy responsible for blocking the Cowboy's freight door, I was not invited to the coffee klatch.

Amazingly, one year, everything changed. I don't recall doing anything differently from year to year. Either the Cowboy must have just accepted that his freight door was closing and I was merely the mechanism for doing it and not the reason, or maybe he appreciated how fast we cleared the rooms when the show closed, allowing his operation to return to normal.

Whatever the Cowboy's reason for his change of heart, from that point on, we were friends.

The Cowboy told me his life story and about all the real estate he had accumulated around Las Vegas. An added benefit to our newfound friendship was that he offered me a cup of coffee.

The offer for a cup of coffee from the Cowboy wasn't typical, either. He would see me and tell me to have a cup of coffee, as—and I quote the Cowboy—"It'll calm your nerves." I suppose he had rattled me for long enough that he may have felt amends were in order, and this was the only way he knew to calm my nerves.

I went to Las Vegas for this event a couple more years after we became friends and enjoyed visiting with the Cowboy over a cup of coffee. I stopped going to Las Vegas for this event, and I didn't see the Cowboy again after my last trip. I wish I had known when it was going to be my last trip and time seeing the Cowboy.

When my children were small and would get anxious, I would use the Cowboy's advice and tell them to "have a cup of coffee; it'll calm your nerves." They obviously did not drink coffee, but the absurdity of the statement made them ponder it long enough to break up whatever the burr under their saddle was. Thanks for that one, Cowboy!

The Career Lesson: Perseverance while doing a job under difficult circumstances may eventually win over your harshest critics.

The Second Career Lesson: When things are tough, have a cup of coffee; "it'll calm your nerves."

27
The DOS

The DOS was the person who was most responsible for my making the transition from carpenter to account executive in sales.

There had been a major consolidation in the industry, and a few folks left the company I worked for to go to the competition. With their departure, there was an opportunity in the sales department.

To replace the folks who left the company, the DOS needed someone who knew the business, knew the commitment of hours, and could hit the ground running. A friend of a friend mentioned my name to the DOS, and he threw my hat into consideration.

In Chicago, the company had recently hired some bright young people who also happened to be new to the trade show industry. These folks were promising and smart; however, after they worked a few weekends in a row with some long hours tossed in, they decided the trade show business wasn't for them.

Imagine walking into this industry straight from college and taking grief from some gruff old laborers or an irate exhibitor at the exhibit hall. With the hours and conditions, it doesn't take long for someone to decide if this business is or isn't for them. New people usually know if it's a good fit for them after a couple of long weekends or a difficult engagement on the show floor.

The hiring goal back then was to balance the mixture of hiring folks from outside of the business with people already in the business who could jump right in. With all the hiring considerations accounted for, I was in the right place at the right time. The goal when I was hired was to bring someone in who accepted the difficult schedule, knew the business, and would be up to the task. I fit the bill, having my experience in the industry, and it provided a great segue to sales.

The DOS talked to the general manager, and upon considering my qualifications, they were both on board to offer me the position. They thought of my transition to sales as an experiment, given that I was a carpenter and untested in an office setting. They were sure of my character but were not sure of my abilities. Even with their indecision, they were confident enough that it would be worthwhile to try. While in the office to grab some paperwork for another show, the general manager asked me into his office and offered me the sales position. The offer came as quite a surprise to me.

Upon considering the offer, my first thought for making the transition was somewhat self-serving. In this position, I would be wearing a suit and tie and attending business meetings and social events where I thought it would improve my opportunities to meet young and beautiful businesswomen. As a carpenter, I was in the convention center during the move-in and move-out, and there weren't many opportunities to meet the people I wanted to meet.

To make a long story short, my strategy worked out pretty well. The first girl I met while wearing a suit and tie happens to be my wife now. The way we met is a pretty funny story, which I shared in my first book, *Dad Lessons*.

My second thought for accepting the new role was that I wanted the challenge of planning an event from the beginning. The idea of starting with a clean sheet of paper to plan an event from start to finish sounded like it would be fun. Setting up events was fun, but selling the event, then planning and seeing it built, was a new challenge, and the more I thought about it the more I liked the idea of making this career change.

I accepted the new position and started on a Monday. I attended an abbreviated training module that included four hours each in the design and graphics departments. With my training completed on Monday, starting Tuesday morning, I was ready to roll in my new career track.

I jumped right in, and my first major event was a major hardware retailers buyers market, working with the DOS. The buyers market is the event where the individual stores send their buyers to stock their stores with the products available at the event from the various vendors. Up until this market, the event had always been conducted in the hardware retailer's warehouse on the north side of Chicago.

As the Market had outgrown their facility, it necessitated the move to a convention center.

The DOS had won the contract for the general contracting services; however, we still needed to win the battle at show site and complete delivery. The best part of having worked this event as my first in sales is that I believe I have worked the most difficult event I will ever work. I am confident I have gotten the hardest event I will ever do out of the way very early in my career. No more guessing if my hardest event is around the corner; it has only gotten better since this event.

The first warning that this event would be difficult came as the manufacturing of our structures in the shop had to be pushed back to accommodate another event. We had a new build and employed some new products that we hadn't used before, and we were concerned even before the schedule changed. The DOS and I joked that our only advantage was that the glue holding the structures together would have time to dry while in the truck on the way from Chicago to St. Louis. It started as a joke, but we found it was more truth than humor.

Once in St. Louis, we learned quite a few more things. The first lesson was the importance of having the home field advantage. We were not at home, and the crew in St. Louis wasn't too pleased with having a group of Chicago people in their town.

As an example, while I was walking in an aisle, a guy driving a forklift with a soda in his hand passed me. Upon a closer look, I discovered it was a can in a red wrapper that read "Cola" in a familiar and distinct white font. After he had passed me, it dawned on me what I had read; however, he was gone by then. Talk about being bold and sly.

To store empty trailers, we had rented a small yard not too far from the convention center. The yard was gravel, with a slight grade leading down to some railroad tracks. One of our truck drivers was hooking up his tractor to a trailer and forgot to put his emergency brake on in the tractor. In hindsight, the sequence of events is easy to predict: no brake on in the tractor, tractor rolls downhill until resting on the train tracks, freight train is nearing on the train tracks, freight train smashes into tractor. Not a great way to start your morning. In fact, I can't even imagine receiving a call and hearing someone tell this to me. The DOS got that call and had to make the next call to the general manager in Chicago.

Another difficult discovery occurred as we walked into the building one morning around 6:00 a.m. Just inside the main entrance of the building, there was a lobby with a feature escalator with glass railings in the center of the lobby. The entire space was very elegant, and the glass railings of the escalator were one of the main features of the lobby.

Unfortunately, someone on our crew had driven a scooter into the glass and shattered the railing before our day had even started. The crews weren't even on the clock yet, and they were driving around wreaking havoc.

The hotel in St. Louis where we stayed still had the old-fashioned elevators that required an elevator operator. It was a neat throwback to have an elevator operator. To operate the elevator, they had a wheel they spun one way to go up and the opposite way to go down. To stop at the right height was an experience; there weren't any gauges or guides to tell them when to stop. They were good at those wheels.

After a while, they even knew which floor you were on. The elevator operators worked eight-hour shifts, and during the move-in, we only met the operator that worked the 10:00 p.m.-to-6:00 a.m. shift, as our days at show site were long. We were leaving in the morning before her shift ended and returning to the hotel in the evening after her next shift started later that day.

We worked long days in a difficult environment, and through it all, the DOS kept his eye on the goal to finish the job and provide a great event for the client. The DOS stayed at show site during the good times and the bad times; he was there and led by example. That show was difficult; but we made it to the open, and the client was pleased.

The Career Lesson: Keep your eye on the primary goal. Don't let a few, or more than a few, difficult situations distract you from reaching the primary goal. Through all the difficulty of that event, the DOS kept his shoulders square, chin up, and eyes straight ahead, and walked into the day focused on the goal.

28
The GM

The GM was the general manager I referenced earlier who actually offered me the job as an account executive in sales.

The first event I worked with the GM was in Kansas City, Missouri, before I made the move to account executive. Although we had a big crew from Chicago working the show, the GM and I were the only ones in the hotel café in the mornings to have breakfast. Actually, I think we were the only ones in the entire café. I don't recall the topics of our conversations, but I do recall that they were pleasant.

As an account executive, the first event I worked with the GM was the second year of a new show. The show had been in a hotel the first year and had grown so much for its second year that it had to move to McCormick Place. The events audience served retailers, and within the event there was a feature area titled "Concept 2000." The year was 1994, and the whole turn-of-the-century thing was ramping up.

Concept 2000 provided a view into the future of retail. There were five stores on each side of an aisle, for a total of ten stores. The area was set up similar to a shopping mall and each store was a thirty-foot-by-thirty-foot booth, amounting to nine hundred square feet in size.

Concept 2000 was a difficult build. The difficulty started with two main entrance structures, one entrance at each end of the main aisle. We used a crane to lift the entrances, as they were large and tall. We then had smaller custom entrance units to each of the ten retail spaces. We also built perimeter walls for the ten retail spaces.

Once our infrastructure build was completed, the individual participants had detailed installations they had to complete in each of their own spaces to display their innovative products supporting retail.

Our first day of installation started at 4:00 a.m., with setting up the two main entrances. The GM warned me the day before we started that the entrances had better be well along to completion by the time he rode up the escalators at 8:00 the next morning. Talk about pressure for my first big gig!

From the start of the project, I was very engrossed in it. The GM had picked several laminates for the walls and entrances in quantities that exhausted the domestic inventory. I had to coordinate with the shop to source the balance of laminate, with it needing to be air freighted in from Italy. Everything arrived in time, but it was a nail biter to get it in the shop and efficiently produced in time for installation.

As difficult as everything had been before show site, the build was coming together quite well, and all the participants were setting up inside their ten individual spaces. The last task we had was to install a laminate floor in the center aisle.

This may have been the first application of laminate flooring. As I recall, the laminate flooring was a new product that was to be introduced to the marketplace for the first time at this show. Our crew started installing the laminate flooring in the morning, and we had a good chance of finishing the installation before overtime started.

We thought we had a good chance to finish the laminate floor on straight time—that is, until Mr. Floor Laminate, who manufactured and sponsored the laminate flooring, started supervising and slowing our progress with his persnickety ways. I was trying to impress on this guy that we needed more work and less talking to finish on straight time. As the product sponsor, he wanted to make sure his product was on display up to his standards. We went back and forth, and progress picked up, but not fast enough.

Just after Mr. Floor Laminate and I talked, the GM asked me how it was going. I shared that we were working through Mr. Floor Laminate's persnickety ways, which didn't sit well with the GM. The GM was very clear when he gave me my walking orders to get that guy the "heck" out of there and finish the job!

I went back to Concept 2000 and told our crew to ignore Mr. Floor Laminate and get the job done. Then I went and directed Mr. Floor Laminate to stay away from the men and informed him that we were not stopping progress to listen to him anymore.

Mr. Floor Laminate was expectedly mad at me.

The floor was finished on straight time, and it looked great—well, it looked great to me, anyway. With the job completed on straight time, the GM was happy to have it completed.

The next week, with the show over and gone until the next year, I was in the office with the GM, and I never saw Mr. Floor Laminate again.

The Career Lesson: Listen to the Boss!

I recall the first internal meeting I attended with the GM. As it was my first meeting, I wanted to make a good impression, so I arrived to the meeting room five minutes early. This was the day I learned that if you were five minutes early with the GM, you were actually on time, and if you were on time, you were actually five minutes late.

The GM didn't waste time, and he started his meetings when he arrived. Lesson learned, and from that day on, I was ten minutes early when attending a meeting with the GM.

The craziest part of the GM's timing for the start of his meetings was that some people just didn't learn how to tell the GM's time. These same people showed up on time per the clock on the wall, but were late according to the GM's time. They never learned to tell time on the GM's clock.

When these folks were late, they received a scolding upon entering the meeting room, as the meeting had started, and then to make it worse, they had to sit next to the GM at the conference table. Everyone who arrived early knew where the GM sat and filled the seats in progression starting with those farthest from the GM.

The Career Lesson: Arriving to a meeting on time may be arriving late, and five minutes early might only be on time. Always be early.

Apparently, the GM was selective about who he hammered, too. I was the nail three times, and each time it was for someone else's mistake. I shared this with someone after the GM had retired, and I was told the reason I took the hit was that the GM knew some people could not take the heat, so he would not give it to them.

The best part about working for the GM was that he spoke loud and clear at raise and bonus time. I have spoken to a few friends and they agree: if you took care of business, the GM took care of you. The conversations were brief and to the point; I enjoyed those conversations!

The Career Lesson: Get the job done, and your boss won't have to worry about you. With some bosses, they won't give out any "atta boys" or "atta girls"; they say thank you when you cash the check!

The last lesson I will share from the GM is that a handshake is a legally binding agreement. I know this, as the GM and a client made a deal and shook hands on it. The next day the client was renegotiating the deal without regard to their previous agreement and their handshake.

From that point on, when this client's name came up in conversation, the GM recited his "a handshake is a legally binding agreement and this client broke it" dissertation. I can't recall how many times I heard this, but I can tell you it was quite often and I know it well.

One thing is for certain: whether the handshake is legally binding or not, one loses their credibility after they give their word, shake hands on the deal, and then fail to follow through on their end of the agreement. Reputation counts.

As tired as I had been of hearing that "handshake is a legally binding agreement" dissertation from the GM, I can share with you that my daughter is even more tired of hearing it from me.

When Madisyn was about twelve years old, she wanted a second ear piercing. Teresa, my wife and Madisyn's mother, said no to the second ear piercing. This debate lasted for quite a while. As they were at an impasse, they came to me to be the tiebreaker.

With their stalemate in my court, I agreed that Madisyn could have the second ear piercing; however, she had to agree to never get a tattoo. She agreed, and we shook hands on it, and then she got her second ear piercing.

At twenty-two now, Madisyn has contemplated a tattoo, and I vigorously remind her that we shook hands on our agreement that she could have the second ear piercing and in return there would be no tattoos, and our handshake is a legally binding agreement!

I'm not sure if this legally binding agreement is defendable in court, given that Madisyn was only twelve when we shook hands, but in the court in our house it has weight!

I will also add that at twenty-two, Madisyn can do what she wants; it's just so much fun for me to say "a handshake is a legally binding agreement" to her! I don't think the GM had as much fun as I do saying it.

The Career Lesson: A handshake is a legally binding agreement, but more importantly, it's your word and your reputation, so keep your word. However, a legally binding handshake might not apply to a deal with a twelve-year-old.

29
The Opposite

The events industry is filled with many unique situations and numerous solutions to each situation. With so many solutions, it is sometimes difficult to decide the best way to move forward.

I have to thank one person for providing me with a great system of checks and balances for making decisions in these situations. Early in my career, when presented with a difficult situation and trying to decide the best plan of action, I would stop and think what this one person would do, and then I would do the exact opposite.

This one person was a fly-by-the-seat-of-your-pants type and was never prepared. If there were a picture of the quote "failing to plan is planning to fail," it would be a picture of this one person.

Some benchmarks indicate the true north; others benchmarks are quite the opposite.

The Career Lesson: Learning from other people's mistakes is a lot easier than learning from your own!

30
I'm Loving It!

I had the good fortune and a great experience to work on a couple of large and impressive corporate events early in my account executive career. Corporate events are unique and in many ways require a lot more engagement with the client than a typical trade show to be able to understand and then create the intended experience.

The first corporate group I worked with was a large restaurant chain that was based in suburban Chicago. On a few occasions, I would walk into their headquarters for the first meeting at 9:00 a.m. and would walk out when the last meeting finally finished at 9:00 p.m. The client was specific about what they wanted and considered every detail and accounted for it while we were in the planning stages.

This organization had an intense focus on measuring and improving everything they did. The scale of the organization was massive, so any small individual improvement they made had a significant impact at scale. As this measuring and improving was in their corporate DNA, they applied this intense focus to their events too.

The coolest part of the meetings at their facility was lunch. The client had a test kitchen in their facility, and we were able to experience the test meals under consideration for introduction or an item served in their restaurants from another country. An added bonus with this group was that there were free fountain soft drinks available throughout their offices. Sometimes the unique things available during twelve-hour days are a welcome benefit.

My second corporate experience was with a major oil company based in downtown Chicago. Their meetings were a little more tempered; meetings started at 9:00 a.m. and usually ended before 5:00 p.m., and rarely lasted past 6:30 p.m.

The oil company meetings usually consisted of one or two clients from the oil company, three people from their advertising agency, a couple of people from their point of purchase agency, and then of course, myself. The meetings were similar to the other corporate event meetings; we discussed the goals of the particular area of business for the event and then created the experience.

Although some of the meetings might extend to 6:30 p.m., the actual oil company clients were not there past 4:30 p.m.

When the clock hit the magic time, the oil company client announced they had to leave to catch their express train; however, we were free to keep meeting. With that, the client stood up and left. With the client gone, the meeting continued with the ad agency and point of purchase people in charge on behalf of the client.

The ad agency and point of purchase people were billing hourly, so they had a stake in staying longer, as they made more money.

The oil company didn't offer free gasoline.

The Career Lesson: Measure what you do and be present to be a part of the important decisions. I still visit the drive-through of that large restaurant chain for a quick meal, and I always love it; however, on the way home I am not able to fill up my car's gas tank at that oil company's gas stations anymore.

31
Shaky, Not Stirred

We had a gentleman on one of our crews who was one of the nicest guys you could ever meet. For the longest time, I could not figure out why we worked him as much as we did, as he didn't move fast or seem to be in a hurry to finish anything. I figured he had a relative somewhere or had some connection to keep him on the crew.

I'll refer to this gentleman as Shaky.

I learned to appreciate Shaky's work ethic upon finally working a few projects with him. I found that if I gave Shaky a task and clearly explained the expectations to him, he would complete the task correctly and in a timely manner.

The key to working with Shaky was that once you gave him the job to do and he started working, you had to walk away and not watch him. If you did stay and watch, you would become frustrated at his methodically slow pace.

We were partnered together on an annual event for several years. Our partnership lasted for six or seven years, and it was always the same job, just a different year. Shaky had a great memory, and he would recall everything we had done the previous year as if it were yesterday. After a while I grew to rely on Shaky, and I really grew to enjoy being around him.

Shaky was the proverbial Tortoise, and he won the race every time with his steady, methodical pace.

Shaky was a consistent person in his pace and accuracy; in fact, his lunch was always the same peanut butter and jelly sandwich on Wonder Bread in the plastic bag that had to be folded and not zipped.

A few folks did not learn to appreciate Shaky's methodical and focused pace. Had those folks stepped back to appreciate everything Shaky did right, they may also have learned that Shaky was a guy who applied himself to do a good job. Shaky was also a genuinely nice guy too.

The Career Lesson: Although Shaky's pace was methodical, the quality of his work was exemplary, and he completed everything he worked on correctly every time. I learned to appreciate the value of his contributions by finally working with him and thus getting to know him, to discover Shaky was a real good man.

32
The Bullet

We had a senior executive whose nickname was "The Bullet." I believe he earned the nickname, as once he had something or someone on his mind, he was like a bullet, straight and fast while focused on his way to that something or someone.

I learned firsthand how he earned the nickname.

While working my first big show as the client's main contact in the Lakeside Center at McCormick Place, everything was going well, and I thought I was doing a great job. The lobby and show management areas were either done or within finishing ahead of schedule.

Every morning I brought the clients the best donuts, cinnamon rolls from Ann Sather, or the pork-filled buns from Chinatown. The clients could not be any happier in the morning to see what I would surprise them with next. With happy clients, what could go wrong?

As I was in the original building at McCormick Place, I was pretty much left alone, as most of the upper management spent their time in the new south building. With it being the day before show opening, the Bullet came to my building and asked me how clean the aisles on the show floor were in the back of the 20 level, or Hall E, as it is now known as.

I wasn't aware of any problems before the Bullet asked me the question. Through the questioning, I became aware that there were challenges with the cleaning crews being able to clean the show floor aisles in time for aisle carpet installation. After the Bullet questioned me about the status of the aisles, I became well aware of the challenge.

Cleaning the aisles on a large event is a difficult task, and when the aisles are full of empty crates, the difficulty is compounded. With crates in the aisles, cleaning becomes more difficult, as there are inaccessible pockets of trash between the crates. When the crates are finally moved, the trash is then dragged, with the crates dirtying up the parts of the aisles that had been cleaned already.

Upon the Bullet quizzing me on the status of the aisles, I had to admit that I hadn't been on the floor in a while to know. Although this was not the answer the Bullet wanted, it was the honest answer. Had I fibbed and said the aisles looked clean, it would have been significantly more difficult for me, as I will explain.

Although the Bullet was asking me about the status of the aisles, he already knew the answer. After I replied that I hadn't been on the show floor in a while, the Bullet went on to inform me that the back aisle was a wreck! He had already walked my floor and knew more about it than I did.

This situation was not good. It was late afternoon when he asked me, and from that point on, I was focused on having that back aisle cleaned. When I started to rally the troops, the back aisle was indeed a wreck. If you are worried about the outcome, you may relax; the aisles were cleaned in time, and the show opened just fine.

The Career Lesson: When an executive vice president can pay attention to the details and walk to the farthest corner of the facility and look for himself, you had better have been there before he was.

The second lesson I learned from the bullet was how to rely on and trust people. As I shared earlier, we had a difficult time producing a first-time event in St. Louis. The people in St. Louis did not cut any slack for a crew from Chicago. It was a difficult event, and it seemed the local team was working against us every step of the way.

After our disappointing experience in St. Louis, the Bullet hired a local person who he knew could help us. This local guy became our guide, or maybe I should refer to him as our ambassador to St. Louis; this might be a better description. I did not know the person beforehand, and upon our introduction, I wasn't too impressed with him.

In the old movies, when the explorers hired a local guide, it usually started as a tenuous relationship. Many times the explorers woke up in the morning to find their supplies stolen and the guides gone. Our guide was an honorable man, and we didn't experience anything like the old movies.

I am happy to say that once I was able to get to know our St. Louis ambassador, I discovered I really liked him. I am also happy to say he was a great benefit to our team. Our Ambassador knew who the slackers were and kept them in check. On our second outing, we worked regular trade show hours, and everything went much better. The Bullet knew what we were missing and made sure we had it on our next show.

The Career Lesson: When you are in a new territory, hire a guide, or an ambassador, just like the explorers did in the movies. Having a guide keeps you going in the right direction and helps to manage the difficult people and places.

When I first met the Bullet, I was still a carpenter with longer hair, and I don't think he was very impressed with me. Over the years, we eventually worked together, and between his softening up and my evolving, we became good friends. Working with the Bullet in the trade show industry was comparable to being an investor working with Warren Buffet, as you learned something new and valuable every time you were with him.

33
The OC

When I met The OC, we worked in the same business group, but we weren't on the same page.

Though The OC was from St. Louis, I don't think that had anything to do with us not getting along.

We became friends when we worked together on a sales pitch and bonded over a common goal. I am glad to have met and worked with the OC, as I learned a lot from him during the process of answering the RFP. The show we were bidding on was an amazing show, and we won the business. It was the start of a great partnership.

The OC is a great sales person. The OC had many years of experience in the business, and he had responded to many RFPs and submitted many proposals. The OC was able to read the RFP and interpret what the client was seeking, and he understood the client's needs. His understanding of the client's needs meant our pitch was spot on and exactly what the client wanted to hear.

I thought winning the business was going to be the hard part, and it was hard, but I found that delivering on the promise and producing the business was even harder.

Our primary client was an extremely thoughtful and well-spoken person. Before every statement was made or question was answered, it was well thought out and thoroughly considered before the reply statement was made. With the client thinking through each statement before delivering it, an occasional gap of silence occurred in the conversation while the client was choosing their words. I found this silence was the danger zone with the OC.

The OC is also an idea guy, and he loved to help the client. When there was that gap in the client speaking, there was a moment of quiet. This is when the OC jumped in, and he would provide solutions to the unfinished client statements. The OC was a quick talker too; he was able to offer two or three solutions in one breath!

The client loved the OC's enthusiasm and all of the ideas he provided. Once we had settled the conversation, I would walk away with having to research the two or three solutions and create two or three designs with corresponding budgets to present to the client.

After a few instances of this, I respectfully asked the OC to allow the client to finish their statements so we could focus on one solution after hearing everything the client had said. The OC obliged, and my workload was reduced by two-thirds. He may have heard this request from someone else a time or two!

The Career Lesson: The OC's enthusiasm was one of his most endearing qualities, and it instilled a confidence in the client that we were on their side every step of the way.

The second Career Lesson is to listen to the client and allow them to collect their thoughts before replying.

34
My Father, Joe Pestka Sr.

I saved my father for last, as he was my biggest influencer and best mentor.

My father was a hard-working guy who loved his job. If you have ever worked a trade show floor during setup and tear-down, you know about the fun times one can have working with their crew. There is a lot of good-natured ribbing that everyone dishes out during the workday, and my father dished out a lot of ribbing, and he had a lot of fun while doing it.

My father gave me some very brief but effective career advice on my first day as a carpenter. I didn't have a lot of time to consider it, as he gave this advice to me while we were driving to work the morning of my first day.

My father's advice to me that morning was "work hard and keep your mouth shut." Then he added that I might get lucky and make $15,000 my first year. It was March 26, 1982; we were already three months into the year. I still remember thinking how great that money sounded to me.

As simple as it sounded, my father's advice was the best advice he could have given to me, and it has served me well. The only time I seem to have any trouble is when I forget to follow the advice he gave to me the morning of my first day.

One thing my father didn't tell me about, or he figured was covered in the advice he had given me, was a warning regarding the range of characters I would be working with. I look back and think he should have at least mentioned that there were some characters who, at the minimum, were from the fringes of society.

I suppose he never mentioned anything about these characters as he didn't want me to be thinking about them. Frankly, looking back at some of the people that were in the business back then, I couldn't imagine bringing my son or daughter into this situation, even if I were to give them a warning.

The first part of my father's advice, to "work hard," served a couple purposes.

Please let me explain.

The first purpose for working hard, and the most obvious, was that we were paid a good wage. In return for the good wages, we were to provide a productive and honest day's work. Sounds simple enough, and I always did my best to deliver. There were a few people over the years that could have used my father's advice.

The second purpose for working hard was that as young man, and as my father's son, I advanced ahead of a few folks when I gained a regular slot on the crew. By working hard, I carried my own weight, and I was at the least as productive as anyone else on the crew. By working hard, I made sure that all anybody could complain about was my lineage, not my productivity. I was not the first person who was related, either, so it was not out of the ordinary.

The second part of the advice my father told me, to "keep my mouth shut," also satisfied several purposes.

Please let me explain this too.

The first purpose for keeping my mouth shut was nobody wanted to hear from a kid about how they should be doing something. In many cases, the tasks these people were doing had been done the same way by the same people for years and years. I certainly wasn't going to help myself by telling them there was a better way of doing something. They would not have listened to me anyway.

I will share that a little later in my career, when I was the lead man responsible for completing jobs on time and within budget, I began to coach people with more efficient ways of doing tasks. As I was the lead man, most of the men on the crew accepted my recommendations, although some reacted with push back.

When there was push back to my suggestions, the reluctant member of the crew usually provided a reply that went something like this: "I have been doing it this way my whole life." I occasionally became a bit of a smart aleck when this would happen. Usually my next statement included how they had been doing the task the wrong way their whole lives. Not a great way to build a team, but I usually only needed these guys for a few days anyway, so I wasn't too worried if I offended them. Either way, if they listened to me or not, the pace usually picked up.

Back to my father's advice. The second purpose to keeping my mouth shut was to not gossip on the show floor. There is a lot of gossiping going on around the show floor, and whatever someone has said will certainly get out and make the rounds.

Trust me, on the show floor every secret gets out. Even when the gossip has been shared with the intent of keeping it confidential, it eventually will get out. I learned, and you should know, that when it comes to talking gossip and keeping it in confidence, the only confidence you should have is to be confident that whatever you have said will be out and known by everyone in no time at all.

The Career Lesson: Work hard and keep your mouth shut, and everything else will fall into place.

My father had committed to working full time in the trade show industry in the midseventies. He entered the business because his previous employer moved their operations to Arkansas. He and my mother didn't like the heat or the spiders and snakes in Arkansas, so they didn't move with the company. Because of losing his regular employment, a friend my father grew up with helped him get onto the crew in McCormick Place, and he went to work installing and dismantling trade shows.

My father knew a lot about traditional carpentry too, same as many of the men who worked at the trade shows. I gained a lot of experience while working with my father on side jobs long before officially working with him as a trade show carpenter. While working with my father on the side jobs I learned a lot about traditional carpentry from him. In fact, many of the skills I learned working with my father as a teenager I still use around the house today.

Truth is my brother Neil learned a lot more from our father than I did. Neil is a much better carpenter than I am, so if you were thinking of calling someone for some help, Neil would be the better choice to call.

One of the most important things I learned from my father wasn't his carpentry skills; it was the art of instilling confidence in your clients.

My father would hear about a side job, and upon meeting with the client he was able to present himself as knowledgeable about the job at hand. As I mentioned earlier, my father, and Jimmy the Greek weren't experts at the side jobs they won when they started them, but they were experts at the job when the job was finished. They bought the tools needed and learned what to do based on their experience. Their clients were always happy about the job they did too.

The Career Lesson: Earn the business with confidence, buy the tools needed, and follow through by exceeding expectations.

Back in the seventies, the trade show business wasn't steady work. When there were trade shows in town, my father made good money. When there weren't any shows in town, he had to hustle a buck with side jobs to keep the money flowing.

When there weren't any trade shows to work or any available side jobs, my father resorted to making a few bucks the same as he did when he was a boy.

During the lean time when I was a child, I would join my father driving up and down the streets to collect newspapers to take them to the recycling center. There was not a lot of money in this endeavor, but when there wasn't any money coming in, this provided enough cash to keep everything going.

Career Lessons

My childhood memories of picking up newspapers to recycle with my father gave me an idea. When my family and I moved to California, my children and I collected newspapers, aluminum cans, and plastic bottles from our house, friends, and relatives. Once we had enough, we went to the recycling center, which was right next to the office I worked at in Anaheim.

Upon collecting the money for the materials we recycled, we then applied the money to the children's college fund. All three of us would go to the bank and deposit the money in the college fund. Unbelievably, the money we earned by recycling covered the first two years of both kids' college education. It wasn't so much that we needed the money; I just wanted to make sure my children could see the value of turning a buck on your own the same as I had with my father and as he had done as a child.

My father also cultivated a good side hustle buying display products that weren't needed after the show had closed. In many cases, the exhibitor would sell all their leftover product for cash so they didn't have to pack it up and ship it back. There were a couple theories on this. One theory was that it was cheaper to sell the product at the close of the show then to pack it up and send it back, considering the shipping cost. The second theory was that it couldn't be sold as new, as it was used at a show, so they manufacturer couldn't do anything with it.

Another theory tossed around was that after the exhibitor sold their product at show site and then upon their return to the office, they reported the product as stolen. The exhibitor had the cash in their pocket from the show site sale, and the insurance check for the company was in the mail. As stated, this was a theory; nobody knew for sure if this was going on.

My father was an expert at finding the booths that weren't taking their product back and were seeking to sell it from the trade show floor. As everyone on the show floor knew my father hustled reselling product, he would also receive leads from the people he knew. My father was a good negotiator, and depending on the product offered, he would find the best channels to sell it for a profit.

One of his annual purchases was from an exhibitor who had a booth full of red toolboxes. My father would actually have to rent a box truck to have enough room to load them up. The toolboxes ranged in size from the simple hand box to the deluxe rollaway boxes professional mechanics use. As my father had to resell these boxes, there were a lot of people in McCormick Place that had red tool boxes. I still have mine in the garage.

The best channel for selling the stuff he bought was usually the flea market. Depending on the day he had bought the product, we wouldn't even have to unload the truck. We would load the tables to the already-full panel truck the night before and be on the road to the flea market at 4:00 a.m.

Before you make a judgement on the flea market, you should know that it is one of the best places to see capitalism in action. If you want a dollar for something, you need to ask a dollar fifty for it, and if you want to buy the same thing for a dollar, you offer fifty cents. Wheeling and dealing is as much fun as it is practical. From my father, while at the flea market with him, I learned to ask for the best deal possible.

The Career Lesson: In capitalism, the price stated is the starting point; make an offer, and you might save a few bucks.

The second Career Lesson: Hustling for an extra buck is a lot of work. It's one thing to show up when you're told to be there, but it takes a lot of ambition to show up when nobody told you to. But the rewards might be worth it.

Back to the ribbing and joking on the show floor. One year we were in Anaheim, California, doing a major trade show, and we had a new account executive on the team. The new guy was very enthusiastic and wanted to do a great job, with this being his first time producing a show on the road.

During the setup of this event, my father and Jimmy the Greek had the new guy searching for the "earthquake paint." They shared that they needed the earthquake paint for some of the units they had built. It was easy for them to convince an enthusiastic new guy from the Midwest who was trying to do a good job. Being from the Midwest, with no experience with earthquakes, it was easy for the new account executive to believe there was a need for earthquake paint.

It's also uncanny how everyone on the show floor knows when there is a ruse going on. At each location the new guy was told that he could find the earthquake paint but that it wasn't there, and he was then told to go to another location to find it. The new guy went to several locations in the convention center to ask for the earthquake paint. Everyone just knew how to keep the ruse going and passed the new guy along, giving him hope he was going to find the earthquake paint at the next location.

I don't recall how the ruse was discovered; maybe someone felt sorry for the poor guy searching for earthquake paint and told him it was a practical joke.

I wasn't part of the ruse, as I was in a separate part of the campus, and I am sort of glad I wasn't in on it for a couple of reasons. The first reason is that I don't think I could have kept it going as long as the ruse lasted; and second, this guy is still my friend. Occasionally when we are together, we still laugh about this.

There have been other stories in the industry of people being sent to get the trailer extenders, column jacks, and I am sure quite few fictitious tools I have never heard of.

The Career Lesson: Work hard and keep your mouth shut. Those exact words aren't applicable anymore; however, the intent still stands.

Closing

Thanks for joining me on this trip through the many Mentors and Tormentors and the Career Lessons learned.

I mentioned in the beginning that there are a quite a few people and lessons I didn't write about.

Writing this book allowed me to relive many fun moments and remember many great people. I hope the people that read the book are able to look back at their Mentors and Tormentors and smile too.

www.ingramcontent.com/pod-product-compliance
Lightning Source LLC
Chambersburg PA
CBHW060835050426
42453CB00008B/708